21st Century Retail Centers:
Context, Culture and Community

21st Century Retail Centers:
Context, Culture and Community

Ronald A. Altoon, FAIA, CDP

International Council of Shopping Centers

About the International Council of Shopping Centers

The International Council of Shopping Centers (ICSC) is the trade association of the shopping center industry. Serving the shopping center industry since 1957, ICSC is a not-for-profit organization with over 75,000 members in more than 100 countries worldwide.

ICSC members include shopping center
- owners
- developers
- managers
- marketing specialists
- leasing agents
- retailers
- researchers
- attorneys
- architects
- contractors
- consultants
- investors
- lenders and brokers
- academics
- public officials

ICSC holds more than 250 meetings a year throughout the world and provides a wide array of services and products for shopping center professionals, including publications and research data.

For more information about ICSC, please contact
International Council of Shopping Centers
1221 Avenue of the Americas
New York, NY 10020-1099
Telephone: + 1 646 728 3800
info@icsc.org (for general ICSC information)
publications@icsc.org (for information about ICSC publications)
Fax: + 1 732 694 1755
www.icsc.org

Copyright © 2009 by the International Council of Shopping Centers. All rights reserved. No part of this publication may be reproduced, stored in a retrieval system or transmitted in any form or by any means, electronic, mechanical, photocopying, recording or otherwise, without the prior written permission of the publisher.

This publication is designed to provide accurate and authoritative information in regard to the subject matter covered. It is sold with the understanding that the publisher is not engaged in rendering legal, accounting or other professional services. If legal advice or other expert assistance is required, the services of a competent professional person should be sought.
— From a Declaration of Principles jointly adopted by a Committee of the American Bar Association and a Committee of Publishers.

Companies, professional groups, clubs and other organizations may qualify for special terms when ordering quantities of more than 20 of this title.

Published by
International Council of Shopping Centers
Publications Department
1221 Avenue of the Americas
New York, NY 10020-1099

Text and cover design: David Hake

ICSC Catalog Number: 262
International Standard Book Numbers 1-58268-077-9; 978-1-58268-077-4

Contents

- 2 **Introduction: Finding a Retail Paradigm**
  Culture and Context as Primary Drivers of Successful Centers
- 6 **1: The Essence of Retail**
- 8 **2: The Irreducible Elements of Making Place**
  Enclosed Shopping Centers
  Open-Air Shopping Centers
- 14 **3: Building on Context and Culture**
  Contextual Factors
  Cultural Values
  Buildings of Our Time
- 22 **4: Asia**
  Ayala Center Greenbelt 3
  Hoshigaoka Terrace
  Nagoya Cloisonné Square
  Taman Anggrek Mall & Condominiums
  CentralWorld
  LaQua Tokyo Dome City
  Namba Parks
- 38 **5: Australia and New Zealand**
  The Chancery
  Harbour Town Gold Coast
  Botany Town Centre
  Canberra Centre
  Warringah Mall
  Knox City Centre
- 52 **6: Africa and the Middle East**
  Menlyn Park Shopping Centre
  Al Mamlaka at Kingdom Centre
  Gateway Theatre of Shopping
  Armada Shopping and Trade Centre
- 62 **7: Eastern Europe and Central Europe**
  The Atrium
  Sadyba Best Mall
  Arkadia
  Stary Browar
- 72 **8: Western Europe**
  Bonaire
  Salamanca Train Station
  Val d'Europe
  Veso Mare
  La Part-Dieu
  Almada Forum
  El Muelle Leisure and Shopping Centre
  Altmarkt-Galerie Dresden
  Les Passages de l'Hôtel de Ville
  Madrid Xanadú
  Emmen Centre
  Bullring
  Estação Viana

100 **9: Latin America**
      Punta Langosta Cruise Terminal and Shopping Center
      Mall Plaza Norte
      Terramall Shopping Center
      Shopping Center Iguatemi Fortaleza

110 **10: North America**
      The Corner at Bellevue Square
      FlatIron Crossing
      Mercado Plaza
      The Grove
      Desert Ridge Marketplace
      Pentagon Row
      Birkdale Village
      The Mall at Millennia
      The Market Common, Clarendon
      Dadeland Mall
      The Gardens on El Paseo
      Fashion Show
      The Shops at Tanforan
      Victoria Gardens
      The Streets at Southpoint
      La Encantada
      The Shops at Legacy
      Downtown Silver Spring

148 **11: The Pacific**
      Queen Ka'ahumanu Center
      Ala Moana Center
      2100 Kalakaua Avenue
      Waikiki Beach Walk

158 **12: The Language of Enclosed Shopping Centers**
      Details That Travel Well

182 **13: The Language of Open-Air Centers**
      The Public Realm
      The Private Realm

218 **14: Building Smarter: Sustainable Design**
      The LEED™ Certification Program Requirements
      Challenges to Sustainable Design
      Centers with Sustainable Design
      Lessons in Sustainable Design

228 **15: Conclusion: Context, Culture and Community**

Introduction: Finding a Retail Paradigm

THE WONDER ASSOCIATED WITH the beginning of each new century affects society in ways that are not always immediately apparent. However, a change in millennia is something even greater.

One of the most transformative changes has been in the design of retail centers, as everyday life in cultures around the globe demands a separate, pertinent and cogent voice. The rational trajectory of shopping center design inexplicably took a sharp turn, actually several turns, from defining the future, to a search back to earlier generations, to a redefinition of the future itself—all at warp speed. In this sea change the retail projects of the past cannot be repeated, while the projects of the future demand new levels of creativity simply to remain relevant and substantial, requiring continual care in order to adapt to unforeseen change.

In the decades since the modern shopping center was created in the United States, there has been a gradual evolution of the prototype from the simple to the sophisticated. Increased research and planning contributed to an improved product. Architects, who used to bemoan the fact that clients weren't interested in building projects of quality or of permanence, saw potential in the extent of the transformative process.

In the beginning, these retail centers emerged without precedent. Most of civilization's other constructed achievements had been based on subtle enhancements to earlier prototypes. This is evident in all of the formal institutions: religious, governmental, arts, sports and even commercial. Evolving ancient Greek temple design informed the Roman works and greatly influenced architecture at the time. The Greek amphitheater found its way into the coliseums of the Roman Empire and, subsequently, to the sports capitals of the world today.

The evolution of the single-room chapel into the barrel-vaulted nave church, to the basilica and the five-nave cathedral, evolved from the Romanesque, to Gothic, to Renaissance, to Baroque and Rococo, touching virtually every continent, with a prototype designed in response to liturgy. Tracing the development of Chinese architecture through the centuries reveals similar refinements that became the new standard. Palace design in Europe, often a study in one-upsmanship, nevertheless reflected the development of a prototype from one generation to the next. The design and construction of town squares, piazzas and other public spaces reflect the essence of community yet respond to the social structure defined by national or local identity.

The marketplace is almost as old as humankind. It is defined differently by the patterns of life in varying cultures. There are the caravanserais of Asia Minor; the marketplaces, haymarkets and high streets of Europe; the mercados of Latin America; the bazaars of the Middle East; the souks of North Africa and the floating markets of Asia. The marketplace is loved because it brings the nuances of each culture to the visual feast in an intense, culturally enriched and understandable way.

The shopping center of the European Industrial Revolution had as its roots a strong, easily articulated community institution. The great retail passages of the central cities were the formal method of organizing merchants under one roof, safe from afflictions of climate, the filth of the street, environmental poisons and rogue behavior. These passages were found virtually everywhere, with large numbers in Italy, England, Belgium, France, Germany and Russia. Many cities had several, often within blocks of one another. They were classically designed arcade structures with multiple levels and formal skylights that were linked to prominent streets and were defined by porticos and gateways. They were notable for the rhythmic repetition of identical structural bays, storefronts, lighting and paving. Passages brought order, security and cleanliness to an otherwise chaotic situation and predictability to the customer.

The passages were a precedent waiting to be exported. They found their way to Australia, but not extensively to the United States, with Cleveland and Milwaukee being notable exceptions. Instead, the United States developed its own prototype, one that grew out of the very distinction that defined a new country and structured its towns on the public square, where every person had a voice and government was transparently accountable. Main Street connected neighborhoods to one another, evolving over time as the major shopping and socializing destination in the New World.

In the late 1950s, the modern shopping center was created in the quiet and calm of Midwestern United States. In retrospect, this was a significant societal shift that occurred as a result of postwar growth for a society returning to productivity after a devastating and debilitating war. People wanted a transformation in their lives, and the suburban alternative to city life offered a fresh start for everything, with new communities, new houses, new roads and abundant open space. The sign that a community had come of age was the arrival of the regional shopping center—a new symbol of growth and identity.

At first the shopping centers were simple in design, often built on greenfield sites. The prototype was an open-air center that had a department store at each end, with all stores facing away from the street or parking lot to form an interior pedestrian environment. Absent was an urban context or a sense of institutional legacy. The centers were functional yet culturally detached from the communities and rarely noteworthy as architecture. They prospered, however, as they addressed every identifiable need and were accessible, convenient, climate-controlled, safe, competitive and well maintained. They provided a civic amenity and hosted community activities. Basic needs were met. But what of desire?

The next generation of centers was promoted as being modeled on the European street. Usually an enclosed mall, often on two levels, with earthwork graded unnaturally to deliver patrons to both the upper and lower levels in equal numbers, these centers provided more creature comforts. Neither stylistically European nor streetlike in character, they were promoted with the exuberant hyperbole of a travel brochure to eager communities across America. It did not take long before communities demanded more than just good merchants.

Evolution of these centers continued through several generations until the passage concept of the 19th century finally arrived in America in a few noteworthy examples such as Simon Property Group's Circle Centre in Indianapolis, Indiana. However, in suburban locations where they are ceremoniously linked with parking fields rather than pedestrian avenues, no urban integration was achieved. Then the Internet changed life in every profession, in every industry, in every place. The now globally connected world instantaneously learns what constitutes the state-of-the-art everywhere—and wants nothing less.

The thesis of this book, supported by several premises, is that culture and context are the primary drivers of successful shopping environments. In economically developing societies, desire trumps need every time.

Culture and Context as Primary Drivers of Successful Centers

In a 1996 ICSC book, *International Shopping Center Architecture: Details, Concepts & Projects,* this writer posited that the fundamentals of shopping center design are internationally applicable, but require national and regional interpretation—and this still holds true. While design concepts have changed, the principles remain.

What is becoming increasingly clearer, however, is that national/regional culture and the specific context that endured it are the primary drivers of successful shopping environment. Various factors support this thesis.

Retailers
In the face of profound change, chain-store retailers have become highly sophisticated. They appreciate that style preferences are influenced by local conditions that require an intimate knowledge of the regional customer. As a consequence, rather than purchasing clothing lines for an entire season, many retailers get daily feedback from stores and adjust orders to meet the near-instantaneous demands of their evermore trendy, sometimes unpredictable, yet loyal customers. Deploying timely buying and merchandising techniques, the stores introduce fresh merchandise weekly, if not daily, enticing the customer to return much more often to keep up with the trends. They know the strengths and weaknesses of their competition—and they react.

Customers
Discriminating shoppers often drive past one shopping center or town center to visit another that more accurately reflects their lifestyle values and affirms their sense of self. They expect that every shopping venue will have roughly equivalent choices of shops and merchandise. They may take convenience, cleanliness, comfort and security for granted. That competing developers produce competitive projects is a given. Shoppers can choose venues that offer similar merchandise but are set in environments that enhance self-esteem. *Pride of place can affect a place of pride.* They want what Main Street offered their grandparents and great-grandparents. They seek authenticity.

City officials

Understanding the potential of introducing retail and mixed-use development projects into their communities, city officials can exercise their authority and influence, concurrent with their responsibility, to deploy this to the public benefit. Their mandate is to create civic places: the plazas, parks and streets that make cities special. They inform themselves, visiting other cities, meeting with other public officials and consultants, and listening to their constituents. And they strive to achieve the best for their respective communities.

Developers

In response to these very real forces, developers have accepted the challenge to help make civic places. They recognize that their long-term investments must adapt to frequent changes in the local marketplace that reflect the evolution of society. Developers can produce prototypes that not only accommodate such change, but also encourage it. Life exists because of change—without it life forms cease to survive.

Sustainability

There is a limit of natural resources and availability of energy. Individual buildings and master-planned projects consume materials, which also require the consumption of natural resources as well as energy to produce and transport them. Sustainable—also known as green or environmentally friendly—building design is being mandated by the federal government, by most states and by many counties and cities in the United States. It is predicted that communities will require retail development in a socially and environmentally sensitive way and will be held accountable to achieving the highest standards.

Architects

Architects, enabled by their clients, can stretch the limits of their imagination and rise to the challenge of producing relevant and sustainable projects that can withstand the passage of time. An example from history is William Penn, who master-planned the city of Philadelphia over three hundred years ago; a city that works effectively today. Penn's neutral and flexible plan was simply a description of the social, cultural, economic and political context of his time as it reflected enduring democratic community values. As such, it readily accommodates modern society.

In conclusion, the built environment of the shopping center reflects the character and ideals of those who make it. Hence, if what is constructed is self-serving, it will be one-dimensional. However, to the extent that an inspired project also mirrors those who embrace a particular place for their retail, dining, entertainment, social and leisure needs, it will sustain a longer lifespan and return greater rewards to both the creators and customers.

1. The Essence of Retail

THERE IS AN OBSERVABLE disconnect between what people often experience in their daily lives and what they admire most when traveling abroad. In the United States, there had been relatively few retail experiences that were not predictable—most were nice, but predictable, leaving nothing to chance, nothing to the imagination. Projects seemed formulaic, repeated relentlessly regardless of context.

Across the country there were anomalies, most often in surviving or revived marketplaces, such as fresh organic produce stands and some lingering remnants of great retailing in the city's center, e.g., Pike Place Market in Seattle, Washington, Reading Terminal Market in Philadelphia, Pennsylvania, and the Farmers Market and Grand Central Market in Los Angeles, California. These are true national gems. But where was the retail theater of the colorful mercados of Latin America, the lively piazzas of Italy, the mystifying souks of the Middle East, London's Covent Garden, Bangkok's Floating Market or Istanbul's Grand Bazaar or its famous Egyptian Spice Market? These centuries-old institutions continually change, making each a significantly different destination on recurring visits. Change begets interest. James Rouse, founder of The Rouse Company, understood this when he developed the festival-market concept. Repeated differently in several cities, the festival marketplace became the closest thing America had to the "touch-and-feel" retail experience enjoyed world over.

For the customer *retail is like fresh fruit*—when ripe, it is alluring, beautiful, fragrant, enticing and mesmerizing. People are attracted to and stimulated by the visual fragrance of new retail offerings. However, when stale, to the customer's eye retail rots quickly; it stinks. Customers are quick to remember when they have been force-fed out-of-date colors, bad merchandise selections or simply bad taste design promoted as good.

How do lessons learned from retailers apply to the design of retail centers? A visit to several global examples of the retail experiences that shoppers frequent when spending their leisure time abroad tells an interesting story.

2. The Irreducible Elements of Making Place

Landmarks, nodes, districts, paths and edges

WHAT ARE THE IRREDUCIBLE ELEMENTS of making place? It is essential that each shopping center be geographically specific, i.e., uniquely appropriate to its particular context. Europeans, for example, create new retail spaces that effortlessly reflect their context, while a more singular culture reproduces what the culture has been historically producing for centuries. Great places cannot be replicated elsewhere without feeling synthetic. In the United States, the design imperative is neither history nor culture, but rather a reflection of the economic agenda. Replicating a Cape Cod village or Tuscan hill town for a project set elsewhere is a misunderstanding of what makes a place special.

Place-making has been defined in numerous ways. Planners and designers schooled in the 1960s and 1970s read Massachusetts Institute of Technology professor Kevin Lynch's urban principles in his book *The Image of the City*. He observed five indispensable attributes of successful cities: **landmarks, nodes, districts, paths** and **edges.** His observation was well established by historic precedent. Whether designing an enclosed shopping environment set in an urban or suburban context, or an open-air center, these five elements are necessary to the making, understanding and navigation of place.

Enclosed Shopping Centers

The urban gallerias, arcades and passages of London, Paris, Berlin, Milan, Brussels and Moscow provide excellent retail precedents. Constructed with a strong sense of arrival, with distinct portal entryways, they have a repetitive order of shops, shop fronts, neutral piers, signage and lighting, including continuous skylights that establish an institutional durability and a timelessness that make them as pertinent today as urban shopping center destinations as when they were first introduced in the late 19th century. Their most important attribute is their civic-mindedness. Their enduring civic presence is irreducible, as if they had always been there. Moreover each place has Lynch's five indispensable attributes: (1) It is a distinctive *landmark* identity that (2) creates an urban *node* (3) in a shopping *district* (4) that provides a *path* to connect adjoining venues and (5) that defines itself with portal *edges*.

Landmarks, nodes, districts, paths and edges

As the enclosed suburban mall flourished in the 1960s, 1970s and 1980s, something important was left behind. Rather than beginning with a sense of civic pride and designing civic rooms, rather than being organized on time-honored principles of order and movement, rather than being rooted in the traditions of retailing, precedent was ignored, and the new vision lacked all the accrued sensitivities of place-making. The rhetoric that described the new "regional shopping center" was carefully crafted, but the product looked nothing like the vision. It would take nearly two generations, about thirty-five years, for the customer to demand more than just the basics. Certainly, the centers were well planned, with proper vehicle access and plenty of parking. Pedestrian movement became a science. Adequate lighting, landscape, security, convenience and promotions were everything a customer might need. Yet where was the attention to desire? Place-making was not fully realized. Great buildings were erected, yet building community remained to be done.

Several notable examples, many of which will appear in the following chapters, are the exceptions. Just about the time Americans were becoming vocal about their preferences for open-air shopping environments, the mall began to approach the urban galleria prototype. Projects like Arden Fair in Sacramento, California, and Simon Property Group's Circle Center in Indianapolis, Indiana, were notable for their strength as retail centers and civic buildings.

Open-Air Shopping Centers

New open-air retail communities have been designed on the model of historic cities using the concepts of High Street, Main Street, urban grid, piazza, plaza or town square. Here, by direct precedent, it is possible to build on an urban framework of landmarks, nodes, districts, paths and edges. For each memorable place, there are *landmarks* that bestow iconic identity and a sense of destination. Within each city or project, there are special meeting places, the *nodes* where programmed behavior ceases and spontaneous activity flourishes. There are individual *districts* defined not only by the character of the place but also by the nature of the tenancies that

evoke a suborder. *Paths* connect each landmark, node and district to another, establishing a framework of expectation. To define the external limits, as well as the internal districts, perceptual *edges* bring visual and physical clarity to the composition.

In the United States, several contemporaneous projects began to bring back a sense of Main Street. Undoubtedly, this followed recognition of the resounding success of two movements in retail development—the creation of the festival market by the Rouse Company and the revitalization and evolution of Main Streets by several developers in historic downtowns. Each brought to it some of the most popular in-line retail mall merchants, who found that their customers preferred to shop in an authentic setting. The days of the polyester mall were over. People demanded authenticity.

When Faneuil Hall Market Place in Boston, Massachusetts, and Harborplace in Baltimore, Maryland, were created in long-neglected historic districts, each brought incredible human and retail energy to enliven a place for community. Each became a beehive of activity. Each brought successive generations of redevelopment to the neighborhood it cultivated. Each of the festival market projects engaged the historic urban framework of the city, embracing the community's traditional values. Culture was the context.

As the reinvention of Main Streets throughout the country began in the early 1990s, among the best were Colorado Boulevard and Lake Avenue in Pasadena, Third Street in Santa Monica and State Street in Santa Barbara. These communities resisted the temptation to become themed entertainment zones or Old Town collections of

Landmarks

Landmarks, nodes, districts, paths and edges

Nodes

Districts

brew pubs and collegiate restaurants as some cities had developed. Instead, they put respect for historic context first, and civic-mindedness resulted. Santa Monica's Third Street invested in an urban design plan to provide guiding principles for individual property owners as they developed a myriad of products, including residential and office spaces over stores. The urban framework accommodated spontaneity, and authenticity resulted.

In the years that followed, several projects emulating Main Street have attempted to capture the essence, the charm and the attraction of these authentic venues. What is important is that these projects depend on the same principles to form the urban framework of community, town and city that have existed throughout history: landmarks, nodes, districts, paths and edges that define our pedestrian realm. Together, these irreducible elements form the structure onto which development projects succeed or fail in making place. Place, at the end of the day, enables community.

Paths

Edges

3. Building on Context and Culture

14

Contextual Factors

CONTEXTUALLY SENSITIVE BUILDINGS ARE generally defined solely in terms of style. This essential foundational framework, however, demands a more inclusive definition. Context is the entirety of forces that inform the meaning and power of place. Far more than the physical presence, it is the human experience that defines and confirms context. In order to properly evaluate context, the following six informants of place must be considered.

1. *Natural environmental forces* of sun, wind, precipitation, temperature and relative humidity influence comfort and, more than anything else, give definition to the buildings people inhabit. It is of no small consequence that the buildings of North Africa utilize centuries-old indigenous techniques to mitigate the harsh, arid climate and provide comfort to people even in the most challenging days of summer. Buildings in Scandinavia mitigate the equally harsh winter, creating interior comfort. It is not by accident that throughout the centuries, cities of vastly different characters have evolved in response to climatic conditions.

2. *Geographic forces* of topography, geology and landscape clarify design opportunity. Buildings are constructed differently in separate geological conditions, varying site contours and against the backdrop of vastly regional landscapes. The interrelationship of human settlements and the natural environment is necessarily different in Jeddah, Saudi Arabia, than in Zurich, Switzerland. Design strategies differ widely depending on context. For example, using landscape to absorb water in arid countries offers a cooling effect or transforming landscape in heavily forested areas to admit sunlight.

3. *Physical forces* of urban pattern and form, density and transit and single- or mixed-use parcels inform the framework of a city and enable place-making. Historic places, designed for pedestrian and horse traffic, continue to accommodate change, albeit in limited ways. Public transit systems, roadway access and servicing issues provide differing options for accessibility. All inform the

process of planning projects in significant ways, frequently driving the design result. The urban context is a prime factor that informs the design of the buildings within it. A new building integrates with its surroundings or ignores it.

4. *Human forces* of religion, culture, social structure, politics, economics and family structure yield unique patterns of behavior. Perhaps no single group of forces defines place more intimately. These factors influence the way people observe their surroundings, how people interpret and understand the behavior of others as well as how and when people participate in activities. They instruct us as to the level and the very nature of that participation. As an example, for people of the Islamic faith, religion influences the act of shopping by virtue of the requirement for women to be discretely shrouded while shopping. In Asia, the social influence of the family unit

may intersect directly in the design of retail centers, where people often shop with three generations in a group, side by side, which requires wider walkways in retail areas. These forces impact the way space is perceived and utilized and, consequently, how it should be designed.

5. *Historic forces* that influence the making of buildings and cities have been a traditional design constraint. Improvements in international transport have made natural materials and products accessible anywhere in the world for a price. Yet traditional building materials and local construction technologies still render style and aesthetic character that have evolved over time to give national and regional distinction to a place. The stone buildings of Siena, Florence and Venice are noticeably distinct from the wooden and paper buildings of Japan's Kyoto or Nara. They are also distinct from the plaster buildings of Mexico or the wooden buildings of the Caribbean. All signal specificity of place.

6. *Market forces* of supply and demand and the competition they engender create opportunity. The challenges of designing in a saturated retail market such as the United States are far different from those in a developing economy that is maturing rapidly. They are further distinct from designing in a developing economy that is experiencing a slower evolution. Developers in Russia, for example, after a slow start in which simply having retail space resulted in remarkable investment returns, now recognize that given the mutable nature of retailing and the increased purchasing power of a highly mobile consumer, they must invest in properties that will endure.

In combination, these forces have the power to influence our lives. When people have the opportunity to choose where to spend their time and money, only the projects that respond sensitively to contextual forces will connect with the consumer on a permanent basis.

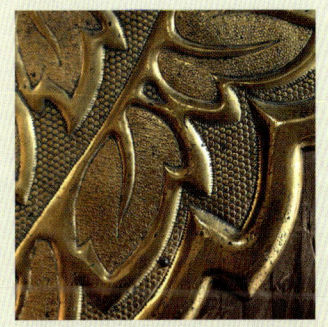

Cultural Values

Cultural values are central to our very being. It is critical that designers realize how a place reaffirms the community sense of self and contributes to individual self-esteem. To understand cultural values, spend an afternoon watching how people utilize a space.

As shoppers, Americans have evolved into big game hunters. They go to the specific venue that has the store that most likely carries the item they need. They may take a stroll afterward if they have been successful and time allows. Shopping is not necessarily a social act—it is an errand. As Asian shoppers tend to shop as multigenerational families, shopping is a social act. Often the shopping center provides many of the pleasures not found at home: protection from the elements, air-conditioning, choices of foods prepared by others and maybe even a clean environment. It is not work, but a reward. What a concept! When did America lose that? When the suburban shopping center drew loyal families from the social interaction on Main Street, a sense of civic life was depleted, and that led to the decline of American shopping streets and city centers. With the renewed commitment to traditional Main Streets across the United States, social interaction has returned to the shopping experience, affirming the power of cultural values.

Several decades ago, The Rouse Company, in a reflection of its own socially responsible corporate culture, recognized that people prefer unprogrammed behavior, not the restricted choreography of the traditional regional mall. With the festival market concept cautiously introduced in cities across North America, Rouse focused on the cultural values that had defined retailers, food purveyors, delivery people, customers and even those who wanted to hang out and enjoy the thoughtfully crafted environment.

Faneuil Hall Market Place in Boston, Massachusetts, was the first development to implement this vision as it utilized historic warehouse properties in a derelict district to bring customers back to the heart of the city. Further development in the area in subsequent years validates the benefit to both developer and the city, which significantly reduced the lease rate to the developer and enabled the project to be economically viable. Harborplace in Baltimore, Maryland, followed, activating the Inner Harbor, which is at the heart of this thriving city's identity today. The conversion of the underutilized industrial port into the city's main public gathering place created the confidence that spurred numerous development projects that have followed in the area: the National Aquarium, the Power Plant, several new hotels and shopping venues, a convention center and new professional baseball and football stadiums.

South Street Seaport in New York City, the Plankington Arcade in Cleveland, Ohio, Bayside Marketplace in Miami, Florida, Westlake Mall in Seattle, Washington, and Pioneer Square in Portland, Oregon, all carefully intertwine the historic and contemporary values of the communities they serve. These inspired, unique projects attract tourists. Each has spawned additional development, further solidifying the renaissance of downtown districts sorely in need of a vibrant street life.

For years, the developer's mandate to the architect has been to maximize the site. What a difference when a developer challenged its design team to determine why it was that those who lived in Colorado, which was the state where the new development would be located, chose to live there. Further, what brought people there to visit? What were their values? What did they do with their leisure time? The speculation was focused on skiing, mountain climbing, hiking, fishing and a myriad of outdoor extreme sports. But, in reality, after a year of intensive evaluation, it was determined that the overwhelming recreational activity of choice was gardening. Gardening! Who would have imagined that?

In recent years, developers have become more sensitive to the need to research who the customer is. It has become increasingly clear that identifying cultural values and providing venues that reinforce them and enable the best self-expression of those values will provide the foundation for the project and will become as important to the project as the area and financial return.

Buildings of Our Time

The challenges of making places that derive from their own particular context, reflect their own culture and enable their own community, are compelling. They require the designer's commitment to research and evaluate all the contextual forces discussed earlier, to learn to interpret them and to create a design that is appropriate in building community. The temptation to ignore local tradition and replicate places known for success and customer appeal is sometimes overwhelming. The proliferation of caricatures of other cultures belies one's pride in one's own culture.

In the extreme, there is the remarkable Las Vegas Strip hotel phenomenon, where hotels are themed as foreign cities, or the retail at Walt Disney World's Epcot, where imitation country pavilions attempt to provide an international experience. Often, these historic impersonators are the result of a market analysis of "average consumer" desires, where they seem to thrive on tourists seeking fantasy experiences. These are effective when appropriate, but the opportunities for this kind of retailing are limited.

Historic replicas are expensive to design, costly to build and challenging to maintain. Developing history-themed projects in conventional communities ignores the forces of history that have produced the authentic structures they replicate and underestimates the design effort required for "simple" replication. On the other hand, the lessons of architecture history do apply as we build unapologetically of our own time. Respect for building materials, colors, textures, forms, massing, shading and shadowing can still produce buildings that demonstrate the vibrancy of the contemporary era.

The materiality of a building evokes a direct and authentic response to the natural, physical and cultural environments. The magic of light at dusk in Miami, Florida, is different than is the early evening sky in Chicago, Illinois. Buildings that capture the essence of an environment do so by contrasting differences in places of quintessentially different auras.

Color is a major factor in the design of buildings. Guanajuato, Mexico, is known for its wonderful collection of polychromatic, thick-walled buildings. Seen as a unified

composition, they are distinctive, creating a panoply of color that is absolutely appropriate in their own settings. By contrast, buildings in Santorini, Greece, are perfect with their stark white walls with blue trim. People marvel at compositions so radically different from one another precisely because each was created to authentically reflect the place.

Even the wall-to-window-opening ratio is based on local climatic conditions, which are married with the technologies that allow windowsills to be wider in one place than another, or formed with a lintel as opposed to a stone arch. They are cues to place, subtleties that make buildings of one place distinctive from those of another.

Shade and shadow define the character of a building form as well as the details that embellish it. Trellises or eaves, canopies or balconies, and window ledges or structural frames create the shade and shadow that bring traditional life to the most contemporary buildings, as they have for centuries.

Asia 4:

22

Ayala Center Greenbelt 3
Makati City, The Philippines

Hoshigaoka Terrace
Nagoya, Aichi Prefecture, Japan

Nagoya Cloisonné Square
Nagoya, Aichi Prefecture, Japan

Taman Anggrek Mall & Condominiums
Jakarta, Indonesia

CentralWorld
Bangkok, Thailand

LaQua Tokyo Dome City
Tokyo, Japan

Namba Parks
Osaka, Japan

The vast geography of Asia is home to many diverse societies, each with deeply rooted cultural values, social patterns and shopping preferences. Home to half the world's population, it boasts several of the fastest-growing economies. The huge territory is often divided into regions based on proximity and cultural similarities, among them East Asia, Southeast Asia and South Asia. While the continent also includes Northern Asia and Western Asia, this book categorizes those areas as Eastern Europe and the Middle East respectively.

East Asia, or what was long known to the West as the Orient, is an area where the uniting factor is the Chinese influence. China, one of the largest and most advanced of the cultures in the region, bestowed its writing system and the Confucian philosophy on countries in the region. This strong cultural affiliation creates similarities among the countries—including a strong respect for ancestors and family and the value of individual industry that translates into distinctive retail patterns—from the prevalence of small shopkeepers to multiple generations of family members shopping together.

The vibrant Asian shopping culture has produced a number of the most iconic retail districts in the world. Tokyo's Ginza district, with its dazzling neons, appeals to a sophisticated and affluent clientele; while Hong Kong's Hollywood Road, where East meets West, draws an eclectic group of domestic and foreign shoppers. These distinct shopping environments reflect both the context and culture of their communities.

For centuries China has advanced its societies under strict rules of urban development, with significant city-planning policies producing the framework for a future development. In such a political structure, a free market economy manages to thrive, mostly on the back of the industrious individual.

And it is the individual who makes retail choices. In Japan sophisticated shoppers have helped to shape some of the most advanced retail centers that respond to both tradition and a generation of trendy young shoppers highly influenced by Western culture.

Southeast Asia includes Indonesia, Malaysia, Singapore, Thailand, Vietnam, Cambodia, Laos, Myanmar (formerly Burma) and the Philippines. The tropical climates, beautiful landscapes and beaches and historically rich cultures have long attracted trade, and today it is also a tourist destination. The cultures have been shaped by the influence of European colonialists: the French in what was Indochina (Cambodia, Vietnam, Laos and Indonesia); the British in Burma and Thailand; the Dutch in parts of maritime Southeast Asia formerly known as the Dutch East Indies; and the Spanish in the Philippines. Religions and languages are diverse, reflecting the influences of colonialism, economic trade and neighboring cultures, especially India and China.

As a result, developing retail in each country depends on an understanding of the traditional local cultures as well as the influences of the intervening centuries. In Singapore, the colorful shophouses, which are spaces containing shops and living quarters, emerged from the work-live culture of the region. Bangkok's Floating Market has been in continuous operation for generations despite the proliferation of urban retail centers, which have forced it to relocate several times. Culture as a condition of the heart is not as easily eradicated as are historic buildings.

South Asia comprises the countries of the Indian subcontinent: Bangladesh, Bhutan, India, Nepal, Pakistan and Sri Lanka. Among these countries, India has experienced an economic boom that is pushing this developing region forward at a rapid pace and will likely be the site of new retail forms as this densely populated region industrializes. Such projects will need to acknowledge the long, rich history of the area; the predominant religions Hinduism, Buddhism and Islam; as well as the British influence.

Project:
Ayala Center Greenbelt 3

Location:	Makati City, the Philippines
Owner/Developer:	Ayala Land, Inc. (ALI)
	Makati City, Philippines
Designer/Architect:	Callison Architecture, Inc.
	Seattle, Washington, United States
Executive Architect:	GF Partners
	Makati City, the Philippines
Gross Size of Center:	300,000 sq. ft.
Parking Spaces:	838
Opening Year:	December 2002

Located within a 4,090,286-square-feet mixed-use complex in the heart of Makati City, Ayala Center Greenbelt 3 is a dining, shopping, entertainment destination. Designed as a four-story, open-air pavilion, it is located in a park that is linked to the center's other commercial buildings by an elevated walkway. Unique goals, such as keeping all of the trees and the integrating nonretail features that include a church and a museum, added a level of complexity to the design. An indoor-outdoor ambience accomplished through the use of louvers, canopies, sloping metal roof plans and generous overhangs alleviates the harsh heat, humidity and strong rains of the environment. Given the Filipinos' fondness for outdoor gathering and socializing, the development integrates public open-air plazas, landscaped courtyards, a chapel and a sculpture garden—all central attractions for drawing events, parties and respite for visitors.

Project: Hoshigaoka Terrace

Location:	Nagoya, Aichi Prefecture, Japan
Owner/Developer:	Higashiyama Yuen Co., Ltd. Nagoya, Japan
Designer/Architect:	Gensler San Francisco, California, United States
Executive Architect:	TECH R&DS Co., Ltd / Takenaka Corporation Tokyo, Japan/Nagoya, Aichi Prefecture, Japan
Gross Size of Center:	140,943 sq. ft.
Parking Spaces:	1,500, in two parking structures
Opening Year:	March 20, 2003

Hoshigaoka Terrace, an open-air lifestyle center, takes advantage of its physical environment and adjacent amenities to create a festive hillside retail environment. Situated on a sloping street, the project incorporates open plazas and a pedestrian bridge that tie the two sides of the street together visually and physically. Each side of the project responds to its own contextual conditions, creating multiple retail environments that have a cohesive architectural feel. Hoshigaoka Terrace lifts people out of their daily routines by creating the experience of a special occasion and sponsoring a design that goes beyond stores to major public spaces, which inspires activity in the surrounding area and becomes an integral place in the city—a destination.

Project:
Nagoya Cloisonné Square

Location:	Nagoya, Aichi Prefecture, Japan
Owner/Developer:	Tanyou Shoukai General Partnership Nagoya City, Japan
Designer/Architect:	Takenaka Corporation (Building Design Department) Tokyo, Japan
Gross Size of Center:	14,556 sq. ft.
Opening Year:	October 5, 2002

Honoring the historic tradition of this particular location as a cloisonné store for over 120 years, the designers created a piece of art where shoppers enjoy the layering of interior and exterior spaces and appreciate the art of the garden—essential values of this ancient culture. The result is a simple yet expansive experience of extraordinary tranquility. Engaging distinctive elements of Japanese culture, this carefully crafted environment connects past, present and future generations through the act of shopping.

29

Project:
Taman Anggrek Mall & Condominiums

Location:	Jakarta, Indonesia
Owner/Developer:	PT Mulia Intipelangi (Mulia Group) Jakarta, Indonesia
Designer/Architect:	Altoon + Porter Architects, LLP Los Angeles, California, United States
Executive Architect:	3HP Singapore
Gross Size of Center:	1,500,000 sq. ft.
Parking Spaces:	7,000
Opening Year:	Shopping Center: Summer 1996 Condominium (2,900 units): Spring 1997

The richness and diversity of the Indonesian culture is vividly expressed in a love of crafts, including a tradition of weaving and carving. The architects carefully researched traditional arts, artifacts and local vegetation, then used the three elements as inspiration for the design of this six-level retail center. A myriad of paving patterns recall woven mats, while window and wall patterns on tower facades reflect tapis fabrics. An abstraction of the historic orchid gardens, which once dominated the site, is reflected in the shape of the building's towers. Water, utilized both indoors and outdoors in the center, references the plethora of islands that form the Indonesian archipelago.

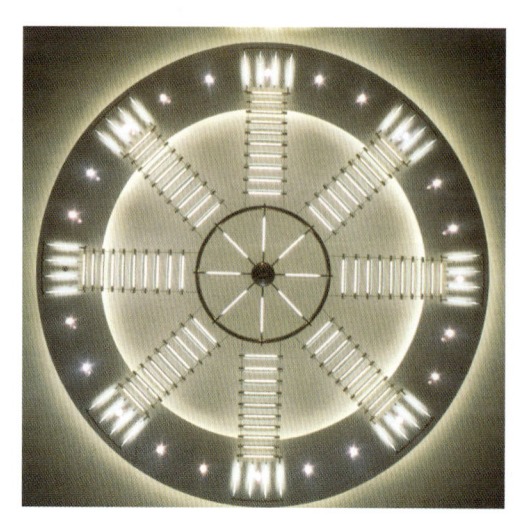

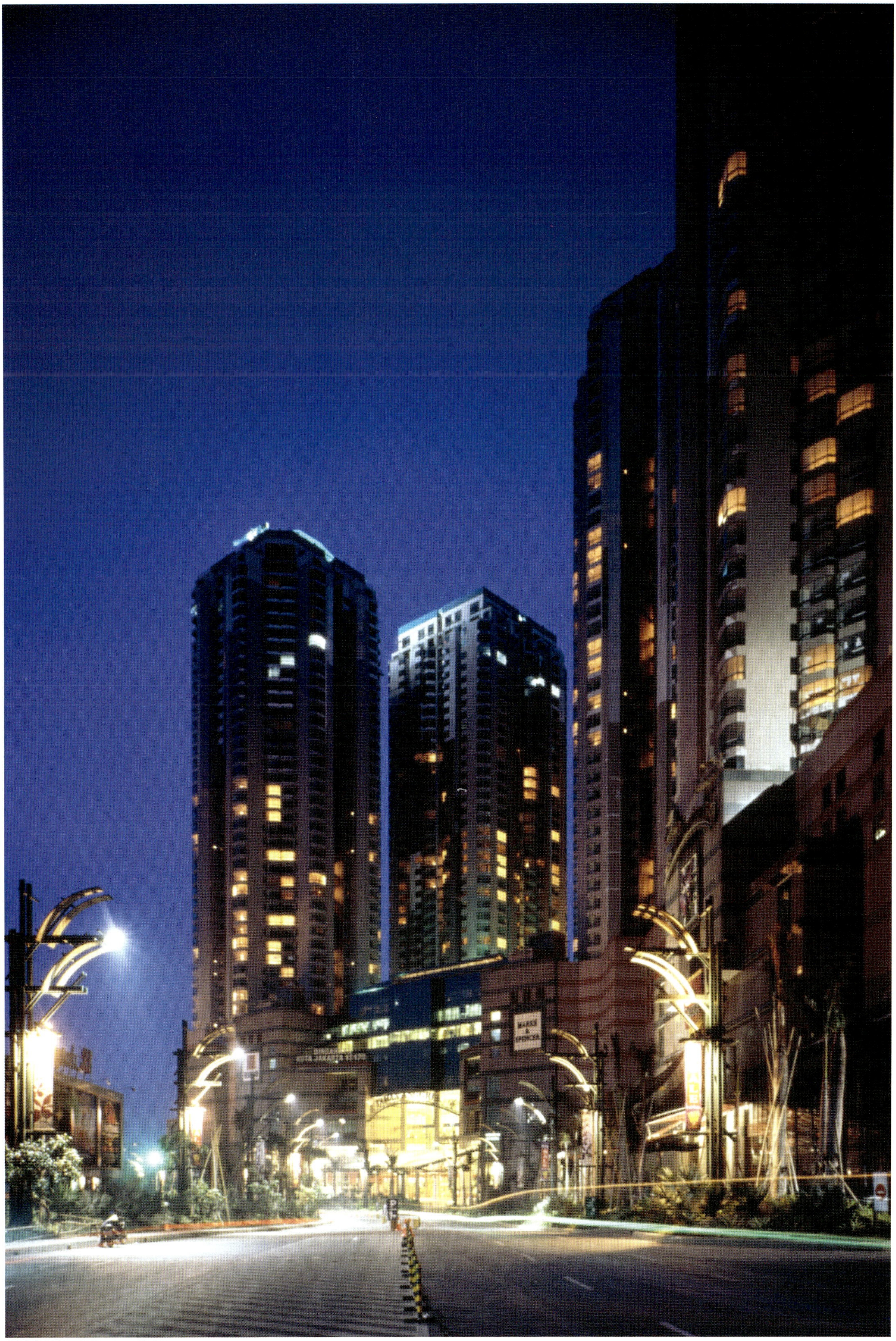
MARKS
&
SPENCER

Project: CentralWorld

Location:	Bangkok, Thailand
Owner/Developer:	Central Pattana Property Group Bangkok, Thailand
Designer/Architect:	Altoon + Porter Architects, LLP Los Angeles, California, United States
Executive Architect:	A 49 Group Bangkok, Thailand
Gross Size of Center:	2,405,573 sq. ft.
Parking Spaces:	5,342
Opening Year:	Shopping Center: 2006 Office Building: 2005

Situated in the heart of Bangkok, the redevelopment of the eight-story CentralWorld draws the consumer's mind from a vertical mentality to one of openness and community. The project expanded social and cultural offerings by adding recreational rooms for activities such as bowling, ice skating and fashion shows as well as grand open spaces for recurring community gatherings, such as the Annual Summer Beer Festival and a New Year's Eve countdown. The visibility of retailers is drawn out by the creation of a "frontage" road designed to work around the challenges of an existing physical context. The contemporary design pays homage to traditional pavilion forms, layering and translucency to breathe vitality into the core of an existing retail arena within the heart of the city.

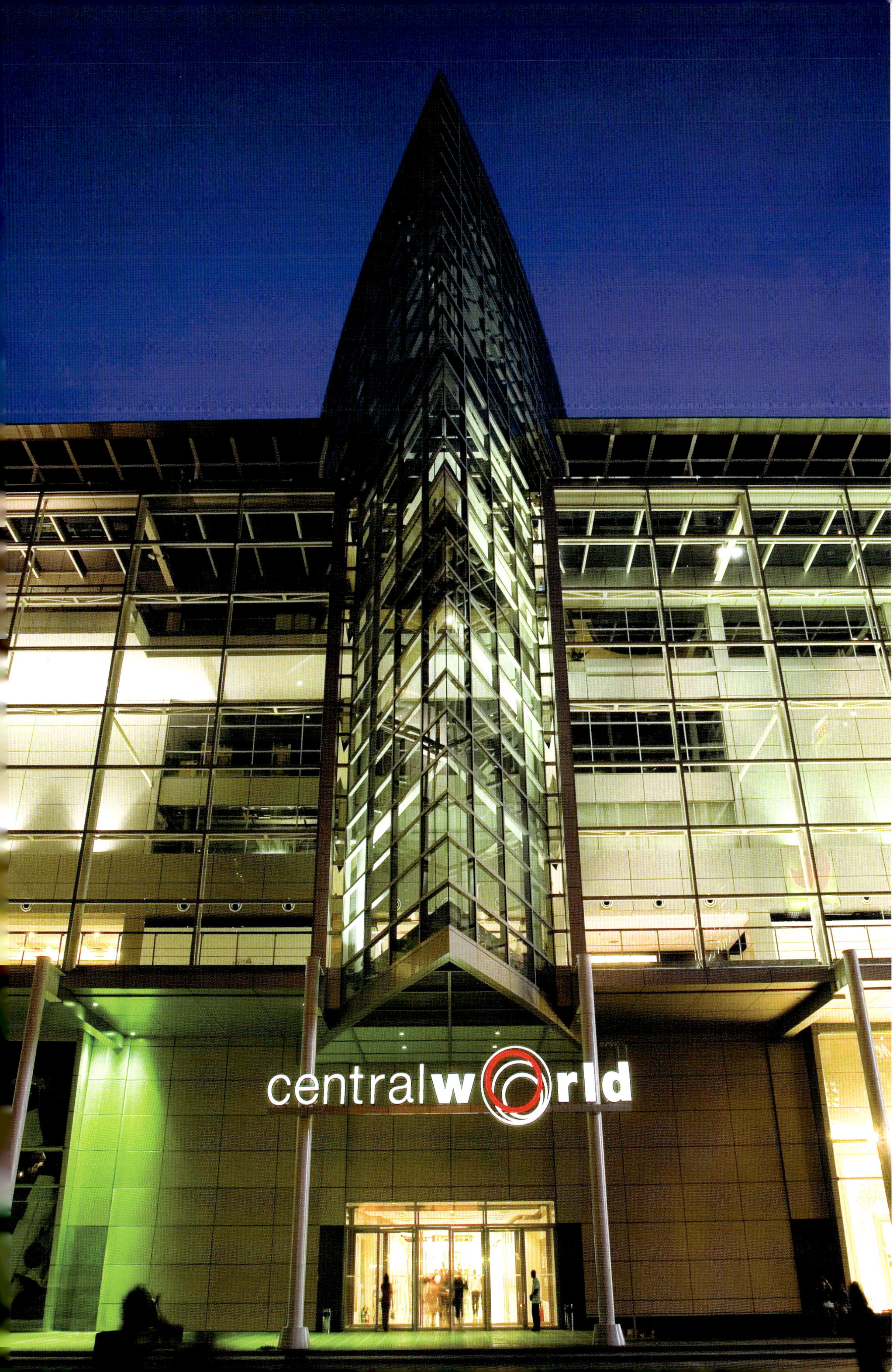
centralworld

Project:
LaQua Tokyo Dome City

Location:	Tokyo, Japan
Owner/Developer:	Tokyo Dome KK, Tokyo, Japan
Designer/Architect:	RTKL Associates Inc., Baltimore, Maryland, United States
Executive Architect:	Takenaka, Tokyo, Japan
Gross Size of Center:	584,000 sq. ft.
Parking Spaces:	200
Opening Year:	May 1, 2003

LaQua takes advantage of its prime location adjacent to the Tokyo Dome stadium in the heart of downtown. Inspiration for the new development complex is an ancient hot springs that lies 1,800 feet beneath the site. An aquatic motif can be found in all of the design elements—from the information directories shaped like water droplets to whimsical aquatic interpretations in the ceiling patterns and handrail accents. The spirited abstraction of water can be seen in the design of the building itself, as its sleek, rising form recalls images of a ship's graceful hull or the fin of a fish. Despite seemingly disparate program elements—from a day spa to the world's first center-less Ferris wheel, from shopping to fine dining—the integrated architecture and environmental graphics create a harmonious one-day escape from the hustle and bustle of Tokyo.

35

Project:
Namba Parks

Location:	Osaka, Japan
Owner/Developer:	Nankai Electric Railway Co., LTD. Osaka, Japan
Designer/Architect:	The Jerde Partnership Venice, California, United States
Executive Architect:	Obayashi Corporation Osaka, Japan
Gross Size of Center:	430,571 sq. ft.
Parking Spaces:	363
Opening Year:	October 2003

A much-needed natural amenity set in Osaka's urban core, Namba Parks is a new eight-level, mixed-use, urban lifestyle center that creates an intriguing parklike environment. The design of the open space is an irregular, organic canyon. At the center of the project sits a terraced amphitheater—a tactile, three-story entertainment space embellished with greenery, foliage and water that rejuvenate the spirits of the visitors. Below the eighth-level roof is a series of green terraces built atop the retail spaces, creating a 2.8-acre rooftop park. This park is an important advancement that reduces the high-density central Osaka's heat-island effect as it infuses the stores and restaurants with nature and open space in this popular new destination.

37

5. Australia and New Zealand

The Chancery
Auckland, New Zealand

Harbour Town Gold Coast
Gold Coast, Queensland, Australia

Botany Town Centre
Auckland, New Zealand

Canberra Centre
Canberra, ACT, Australia

Warringah Mall
Brookvale, Sydney, NSW, Australia

Knox City Centre
Melbourne, Australia

AUSTRALIA IS THE WORLD'S smallest continent but the sixth largest country, slightly smaller than the 48 contiguous United States. The population is highly urbanized, concentrated along the eastern and southern coasts. While New Zealand is technically part of Polynesia, the country shares many of the same historical and cultural traits as Australia, and this background has shaped the retail developments of both countries in similar ways.

Place names along Australia's coast indicate the influence of the early Dutch, French and British explorers as well as the Aboriginal natives, and today the country is fully multicultural, its citizens emigrating from nearly every country and practicing almost every religion and lifestyle. With strong ties to the Anglo–Celtic culture of early settlers and recent influences from American popular culture, Australia's unique environment and indigenous culture shape its national identity and retail patterns.

New Zealanders, geographically isolated like their Australian neighbors, want to stay current with the rest of the world at the same time that they protect their rich natural environment and powerful native Maori culture.

While retail development has been limited by the relatively small number of local retail formats and operators and by significant governmental protectionism to deny offshore access of retailers to local markets, the most sophisticated regional developers and architects nevertheless apply merchandising creativity to the situations with which they are faced. They have produced some of the most interesting retail places, with combined uses thought unrealistic in the United States and Europe—until now.

Project:
The Chancery

Location:	Auckland, New Zealand
Owner/Developer:	Chancery Limited Auckland, New Zealand
Designer/Architect:	IGNITE Limited Auckland, New Zealand
Gross Size of Center:	53,163 sq. ft.
Parking Spaces:	228
Opening Year:	December 2000

Carefully wedged onto a small, sloping, triangular urban site, this retail complex creates a hub of activity that invites people to pause and interact with one another. Four levels of residential space located above the retail stores help to generate a busy 18-hour-a-day life cycle that responds to the New Zealanders' cultural inclination to socialize on the street with one's "mates." While shop fronts actuate each of the three streets they face, pathways from the three corners bring customers past shops to a central piazza. Impressive high shop fronts and street furnishings provide an intimately scaled shopping and dining experience.

41

Project:
Harbour Town Gold Coast

Location:	Gold Coast, Queensland, Australia
Owner/Developer:	Lewis Land Group of Companies/ ING Real Estate Sydney, New South Wales, Australia
Designer/Architect:	The Buchan Group Brisbane, Queensland, Australia
Gross Size of Center:	500,000 sq. ft.
Parking Spaces:	3,000
Opening Year:	December 1999; Expansion: 2003

Harbour Town Gold Coast serves both tourists and local residents of the Gold Coast, Australia's leading tourist destination and home to places such as Surfers Paradise. The project integrates banking and postal facilities, a major medical center, fitness center, and health and beauty salons along with a major cinema complex, international restaurants and national and internationally known outlet stores. Buildings with colorful facades that contrast against brilliant blue skies are designed to respond to Gold Coast's climate and geography. Palm trees line mosaic walkways that meander through the center. A loyalty program for local residents and a tourist VIP Program inspire local residents to value the shopping experience in a place they already call home and allow tourists to feel at home.

43

Project Name:
Botany Town Centre

Location:	Auckland, New Zealand
Owner/Developer:	AMP Henderson Global Investors Auckland, New Zealand
Design Architect:	Altoon + Porter Architects, LLP Los Angeles, California, United States
Executive Architect:	Hames Sharley Auckland, New Zealand
Gross Size of Center:	520,122 sq. ft.
Parking Spaces:	2,749
Opening Year:	Large Format Shops: September 20, 2000 Town Center: May 6, 2001

The often-polarized elements of urban life and the natural environment were sensitively combined through a center design that pays homage to the preservation of community, history, culture and flora and provides a thoughtful framework that has become retail success. The design juxtaposes indigenous art, integrating Maori spiritual elements with parks, gardens, and waterways. Building orientation; landscaping; heating, ventilating and air-conditioning (HVAC) systems; and daylighting partners with spaces that range from fully enclosed to partially protected—in consideration of the moderate, yet wet climate—are a direct response to sustainability concerns. Botany Town Centre is a commercially vibrant center existing harmoniously within the context of environment and spirit that is essential to the community.

45

Project:
Canberra Centre

Location:	Canberra, ACT, Australia
Owner/Developer:	QIC Real Estate
	Brisbane, Queensland, Australia
Designer/Architect:	Daryl Jackson Alastair Swayn Pty Ltd.
	Canberra, ACT, Australia
Gross Size of Center:	613,758 sq. ft.
Parking Spaces:	3,300
Opening Year:	October 31, 1989;
	Expansion: November 11, 2002

A recent renovation and expansion reassert Canberra Centre as Canberra's premiere shopping destination. The consolidation integrates a supermarket, stores, office, car-park decks and stores from three disconnected city blocks into one unified complex in a two-story arcade along Ainslie Avenue, a street that divides the city center. Adjacent retail areas were also upgraded and refurbished to provide seamless links with the new project. Ainslie Avenue was closed to vehicular traffic to become a pedestrian street that has reclaimed the public realm. The center supports the revitalization of civic life with the incorporation of an exciting urban design, the use of natural light and the introduction of a number of new retail businesses to Canberra.

47

Project:
Warringah Mall

Location:	Brookvale, Sydney, NSW, Australia
Owner/Developer:	AMP Henderson Global Investors Australia and New Zealand
Design Architect:	Phases 1 and 2: Altoon + Porter Architects, LLP Los Angeles, California, United States
Executive Architect:	Phase 1: Roger Thrum & Associates Sydney, Australia Phase 2: Woods, Bagot Sydney, Australia
Gross Size of Center:	1,197,943 sq. ft.
Parking Spaces:	4,700
Opening Year:	Phase 1: Summer 1998 Phase 2: Summer 1999

Open enough to reveal the richness of the flora and fauna of the region, the center is structured enough to give order to the circulation pattern. Taking advantage of the benign climate, the design is a progression of space experiences—from fully open air to trellised, from covered yet open, to covered and enclosed, with and without air-conditioning—utilizing a series of materials from fabric to glass. Abstractions of architectural icons of Sydney's beaches and deserts further integrate the mall with its environment. A series of indoor-outdoor shopping "neighborhoods," reflecting the casual lifestyle of the Northern Beaches, are linked to the new center court with glass-covered galleries.

49

Project:
Knox City Centre

Location:	Melbourne, Australia
Owner/Developer:	AMP Henderson Global Investors Australia and New Zealand
Designer/Architect:	Altoon + Porter Architects, LLP Los Angeles, California, United States
Executive Architect:	Hames Sharley Melbourne, Australia
Gross Size of Center:	1,450,000 sq. ft.
Parking Spaces:	1,300
Opening Year:	Spring 2003

Knox City's location between Melbourne and the Dandenong Ranges provided a rich pictorial and metaphorical vocabulary for the designers. The design engages the customer by offering an architectural evocation of the Australian lifestyle. Six separate areas, each with a memorable name and visual personality, guide shoppers throughout the center and offer distinct merchandising opportunities. Each area finds expression in native timbers and lodge forms, in the palettes and patterns of the vineyards, in the broad verandahs and lawns of a town square and in the bright lights and energy of an urban scene. As a result visitors enjoy a range of leisure options and a marked sense of place that is as diverse and authentic as the region itself.

51

6. Africa and the Middle East

Menlyn Park Shopping Centre
Pretoria, Gauteng, Republic of South Africa

Al Mamlaka at Kingdom Centre
Riyadh, Kingdom of Saudi Arabia

Gateway Theatre of Shopping
Umhlanga Ridge, Durban, Republic of South Africa

Armada Shopping and Trade Centre
Ankara, Turkey

THE MIDDLE EAST IS a broad territorial concept that often includes the regions of Southwest Asia from Turkey to the Iranian border, the Arabian Peninsula and North Africa. Despite a diversity of ethnicity and culture, these countries are linked by their shared history and for most, by the Islamic religion. Not all the countries of the region are actively developing new retail centers. Those that are doing so forge new ground as designers and find inventive ways of responding to the cultural sensitivities.

Across the region, there is a long history of trade, from the early caravanserai to the later bazaars and souks where retail negotiations are still a fine art and this tradition has its influences. While the Arab countries and the Turks both enjoy the barter of the bazaar, the Turkish economy is more closely aligned with Europe and the new centers reflect those aspirations. At the same time, in petroleum-rich countries such as Saudi Arabia and Dubai, new projects are testament to the cultural desire for modernized shopping alternatives.

In South Africa, the European influences, the abundant supply of resources and the energy of the recently enfranchised native population have combined to keep the economy strong in the major cities: Cape Town, Port Elizabeth, Durban, Pretoria and Johannesburg.

Project:
Menlyn Park Shopping Centre

Location:	Pretoria, Gauteng, Republic of South Africa
Owner/Developer:	Old Mutual Life Assurance Company of South Africa Cape Town, Western Cape, Republic of South Africa
Designer/Architect:	Bild Architects Pretoria, Gauteng, Republic of South Africa
Gross Size of Center:	1,271,562 sq. ft.
Parking Spaces:	544 (2,044 parking spaces added in renovation)
Opening Year:	October 1983; Expansion date: February 2001

The renovation of Pretoria's Menlyn Park Shopping Centre nearly doubled the size of this popular shopping center, transforming it into a dazzling shopping and entertainment experience. Highly experiential design is complemented by a palette of bright, upbeat, jubilant colors and striking patterns celebrating the ambience of Africa. The use of new lighting techniques, powerful sculptural graphics and a carefully planned tenant design criterion has many international retailers vying for inclusion on the center's growing tenancy waiting list. Menlyn Park offers South Africa retail solutions, launching "world firsts" both in terms of sales and new experiences for shoppers, including the country's first drive-in movie theater.

55

Project:
Al Mamlaka at Kingdom Centre

Location:	Riyadh, Kingdom of Saudi Arabia
Owner/Developer:	Kingdom Holding Co. and Trade Centre Company Limited Riyadh, Kingdom of Saudi Arabia
Design Architect:	Altoon + Porter Architects, LLP Los Angeles, California, United States
Executive Architect:	Omrania, Inc. Cairo, Egypt and Riyadh, Saudi Arabia
Gross Size of Center:	650,000 sq. ft.
Parking Spaces:	Center: 2,000; Other: 1,000
Opening Year:	November 15, 2001

With special concern to respect the tenets of the Islamic faith, this three-level center provides a retail environment that allows female shoppers to abandon the *abayeh* and engage freely with the merchandise, protected from public view. Inspired by traditional Arabic domestic architecture, the designers placed a "veil" on the building itself, providing the necessary visual protection. A separate porte cochere at the third level delivers women directly to the Women's Kingdom. There, a beauty salon and fitness center, a business center, cafes, restaurants, two department stores and shops all focus on women's needs. Natural light fills the space, while the heat from the harsh desert sun is filtered by a ceiling of layered materials that uses traditional methods of screening in a contemporary way.

57

Project:
Gateway Theatre of Shopping

Location:	Umhlanga Ridge, Durban, Republic of South Africa
Owner/Developer:	Old Mutual Property Group Cape Town, Western Cape, Republic of South Africa
Designer/Architect:	RTKL Associates Baltimore, Maryland, United States
Executive Architect:	Johnson Murray Architects Durban, KwaZulu-Natal, Republic of South Africa
Gross Size of Center:	3,443,200 sq. ft.
Parking Spaces:	7,500
Opening Year:	September 27, 2001

The Gateway Theatre of Shopping provides the residents of Durban, along the Umhlanga Ridge in South Africa, with 1.4 million square feet of shops, restaurants and entertainment venues in a form that combines a traditional mall with the open-air spaces and the infrastructure of a new town center. An essential goal of the design was to divide the vast shopping center into different districts through environmental design themes. Five separate entrances, easily distinguishable by their interior motifs, lead to different parts of the mall. Umhlanga's main boulevard leads to Gateway's main entrance, where patrons are greeted with a large roundabout with an interactive fountain and light shows.

59

Project:
Armada Shopping and Trade Centre

Location:	Ankara, Turkey
Owner/Developer:	Sogutozu Construction and Management Inc. Ankara, Turkey
Designer/Architect:	GMW Architecture and Consulting Ltd. Co. London, United Kingdom
Gross Size of Center:	1,076,426 sq. ft.
Parking Spaces:	3,000
Opening Year:	September 28, 2002

Armada means the flagship of a naval flotilla, inspired by Ankara's location on what was once an inner sea. The glass-covered complex is a city within a city, with the mall block resembling a cruiser. It sits on property that is visible from most of Ankara, which proved to be an important criterion in the design of the six-story shopping center that features 153 shops, 21 restaurants and 11 movie halls alongside a 21-story office building. Because of its location, the urban site is suitable for different expansions of shopping, entertainment and business life. The upscale tenant profile includes international clothing stores and restaurants. The hypermarket floor provides services such as a dry cleaning center, a bank, a photo studio and a hypermarket, among others. The lower floor serves children, home decor, hobbies and personal care. There is also a textile and ready-to-wear floor as well as a food court.

61

7. Eastern Europe and Central Europe

The Atrium
Moscow, Russian Federation

Sadyba Best Mall
Warsaw, Poland

Arkadia
Warsaw, Poland

Stary Browar
Poznan, Poland

The regions of Eastern and Central Europe can be variably defined. In terms of current retail activity, many interesting projects are being developed in what was the former Eastern Bloc, countries that were part of the Soviet Union and its satellites, including Russia, Poland, the Czech Republic, Slovakia, Hungary and the Balkans. These countries each have a distinctive history and a rich cultural heritage that is being actively invoked as they re-enter the commercial marketplace.

Russia, the largest and most powerful country in the region, is itself a hybrid state created out of the cultures of multiple nationalities over centuries. However, the Russian culture of an earlier epoch provides not only the collective memory of elegance and sophistication, but also a stunning architectural history that includes one of the world's grand department stores, the GUM, which is made up of three multilevel malls. With the return of capitalism, Russian shoppers are eager to enjoy the diversity of quality goods that were unavailable for years, and they find the well-stocked, modern retail centers based on Western models a strong draw.

Other countries such as Poland, Hungary and the Czech Republic are eagerly catching up with the shopping center industry, too. Designers of retail centers in these countries draw on the colorful local history, architecture and culture to create new retail formats that capitalize on the centuries-old traditions of the outdoor markets and small shops as well as the 21st-century retail forms that have quickly been introduced.

Project:
The Atrium

Location:	Moscow, Russian Federation
Owner/Developer:	Engeocom, Inc.
Designer/Architect:	Altoon + Porter Architects, LLP
	Los Angeles, California, United States
Executive Architect:	MosProject 2
	Moscow, Russian Federation
Gross Size of Center:	280,000 sq. ft.
Parking Spaces:	1,000
Opening Year:	Summer 2002

Located on the Garden Ring, one of three rings on which the city of Moscow was developed, this highly contextual project responds to the region's harsh physical climate and to the cultural context of the urban site in Moscow. The building has become an icon that contributes to the historic character of the district. Design details resonate with Moscow's distinctive indigenous architecture, and the highly chromatic facades provide an inviting contrast to the often snowy streets of the city. Inside, the Winter Garden offers a respite from the climate and creates a sense of order for the center.

65

Project:
Sadyba Best Mall

Location:	Warsaw, Poland
Owner/Developer:	Sadyba Center S.A.
	Warsaw, Poland
Designer/Architect:	Pawel W. Gralinski
	Warsaw, Poland
Gross Size of Center:	279,864 sq. ft.
Parking Spaces:	1,015
Opening Year:	September 2000;
	Expansion: August 2004

Sadyba Best Mall is located on a main thoroughfare in the densely populated Mokotov district in Warsaw, which has the highest average per capita income and level of education in the market catchments, making it ideal for a regional mall. Surrounded by the district's residential complexes, the three-level center has broad public appeal, boasting fashion shops, a supermarket, a food court and recreational venues, such as a 20-lane bowling alley and cinemas, including the first IMAX theater in central Europe. The careful design of the exterior facades presents a variety of shapes, colors and small-scale details that enhance the surrounding neighborhood and help make Sadyba a desirable community gathering place.

67

Project:
Arkadia

Location:	Warsaw, Poland
Owner/Developer:	Simon-Ivanhoe/Groupe BEG
	Paris, France
Designer/Architect:	RTKL
	Baltimore, Maryland, United States
Executive Architect:	BEG Ingenierie
	Orleans, France
Gross Size of Center:	3,089,242 sq. ft.
Parking Spaces:	4,000
Opening Year:	October 2004

Arkadia celebrates Polish culture with charming visual references to traditional folk legends, the famous Vistula River and Copernicus, the noted Polish astronomer. Inside the grand civic space, the design pays homage to the country's proud heritage with displays highlighting eight historic cities, including Warsaw. This paean to Polish culture is reinforced by the superb workmanship of the local craftspeople, who seized the opportunity to demonstrate their exceptional skills in decorative metal, stone and plaster work and mural painting. Given its emotion-laden location—it is on the site of the historic point of departure for the Warsaw Jews who were sent to the concentration camps—the developers dedicated an expanse of lawn, set back from the bustle of the traffic, to the memory of the persecutions and the destruction of the city.

69

Project: Stary Browar

Location:	Poznan, Poland
Owner/Developer:	Fortis Sp. z o.o. Poznan, Poland
Designer/Architect:	Studio ADS Sp. z o.o. Poznan, Poland
Gross Size of Center:	699,654 sq. ft.
Parking Spaces:	400
Opening Year:	November 6, 2003

The deteriorating Hugger Brothers brewery buildings in the heart of Poznan in western Poland have been revived as an elegant contemporary center for shopping, art and civic functions. A careful renovation gave the vintage malt house, boiler room, storage cellar and villa practical new functions with an architecture that honors the 19th-century style. New buildings are integrated to create a coherent design that fully belongs to its context. In addition to introducing state-of-the-art European shopping, the center created a popular venue for cultural and artistic events in inventive new settings such as the former Malt House, which has a gallery that hosts art exhibits, theater and dance performances and cinema showings. With its new image and attractions, the center has sparked new development in the city center.

71

Western Europe

8.

Bonaire
Aldaia, Valencia, Spain

Salamanca Train Station
Salamanca, Spain

Val d'Europe
Marne-la-Vallée, France

Veso Mare
Patras, Greece

La Part-Dieu
Lyon, France

Almada Forum
Almada, Portugal

El Muelle Leisure and Shopping Centre
Las Palmas de Gran Canaria, Las Palmas, Spain

Altmarkt-Galerie Dresden
Dresden, Germany

Les Passages de l'Hôtel de Ville
Boulogne-Billancourt, France

Madrid Xanadú
Arroyomolinos, Madrid, Spain

Emmen Centre
Emmenbrücke, Switzerland

Bullring
Birmingham, United Kingdom

Estação Viana
Viana do Castelo, Portugal

IN MANY WAYS, WESTERN Europe is the prime source for ideas about what makes for a rich shopping experience. From the open-air markets of every provincial town across France, Italy and the Iberian Peninsula, to the market towns of Germany and England, to the grand *magasins* of Paris, to the flea market on Portbello Road in London, the specialty shops on the Via Spiga in Milan or the restaurants on Las Ramblas in Barcelona—these are the iconic images of retail.

Introducing innovative new retail forms to sophisticated Western European shoppers requires a thorough understanding of the unique characteristics of each market, including the different cultural values placed on food and clothing, workplace protocols and hours of operation. At the same time, there is a lively interest in the latest fashion, technology and global trends among these educated, worldly shoppers that will support new retail formats. The new formats respect the historic context and landscape while recognizing the differences in both national and regional cultures, with centers that speak the local language architecturally and programmatically.

In Western Europe, where retail has been a mature industry for generations, a current trend is to expand the reach of retail to include diverse other uses. Integration of highly utilized and well-maintained public-transit systems allows the effective inclusion of residential, office, leisure, recreation, entertainment, dining, cultural, public health and civic uses. Highly urban in character, the new retail of Western Europe tends to be reflective of past, present and future values.

Project:
Bonaire

Location:	Aldaia, Valencia, Spain
Owner/Developer:	Riofisa and Rodamco, Madrid, Spain
Designer/Architect:	Idom Ingenieria, Madrid, Spain
Gross Size of Center:	1,500,000 sq. ft.
Parking Spaces:	6,000
Opening Year:	May 2001

Located near Valencia, Aldaia has long been known as a place to escape on weekends and enjoy the "good air." The Bonaire development builds on the notion of respite with a mixed-use complex offering a variety of entertainment and retail options. Four distinctive open-air spaces arrayed in a circular plan include: a fashion section that features a dignified, classical architecture; a home section with a comfortable, welcoming style; a leisure section that links to an internal food court and a 16-screen cinema; and a children's fashion and retail entertainment section. The center is an accessible, distinctive place that embraces the sound, color and seaside ambience of the Mediterranean to deliver value, diversity and a sense of the local community.

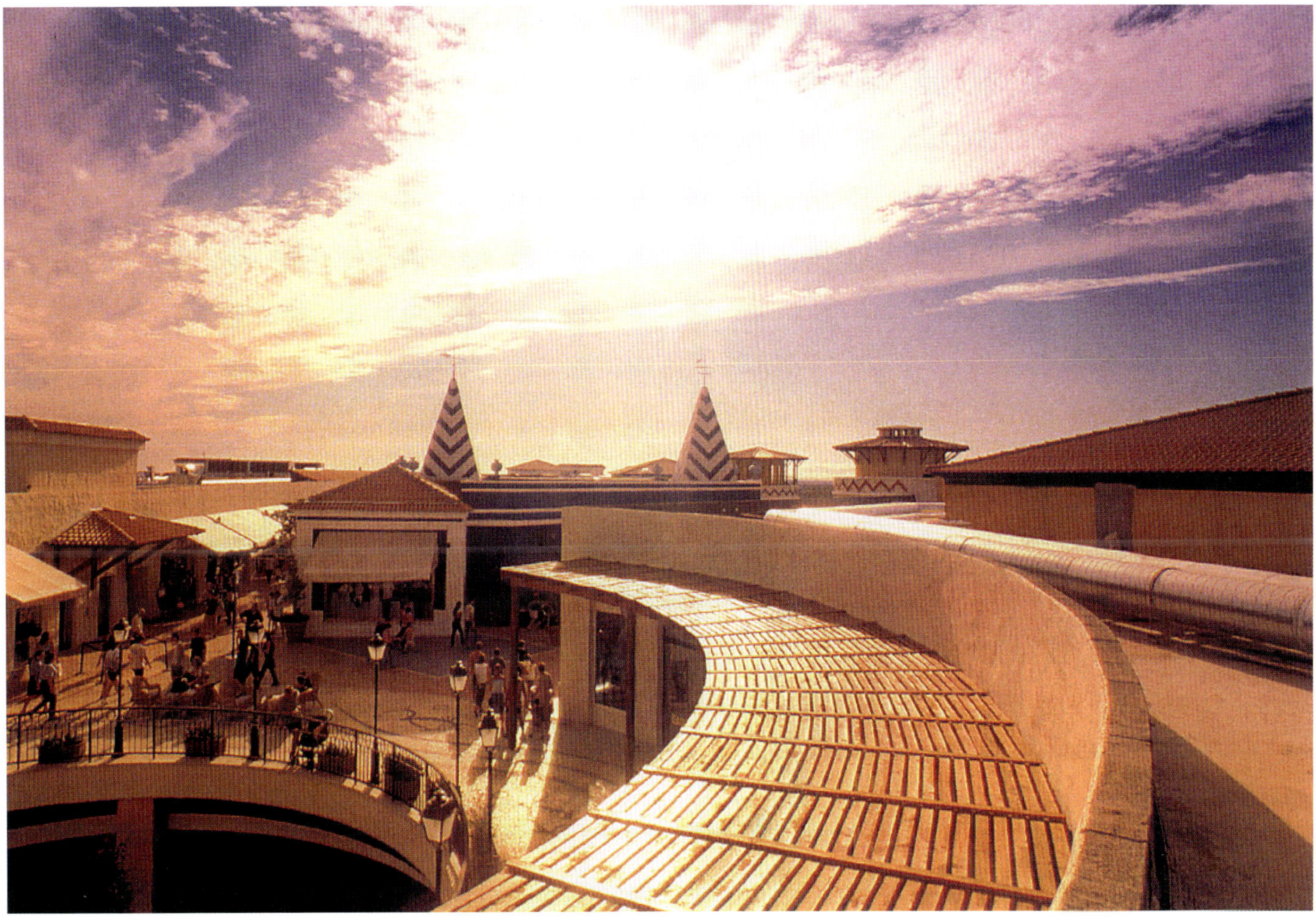

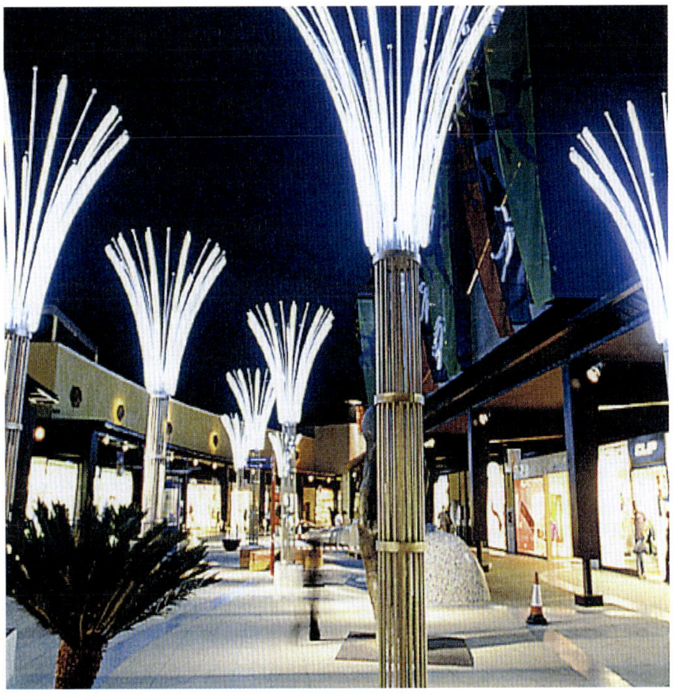

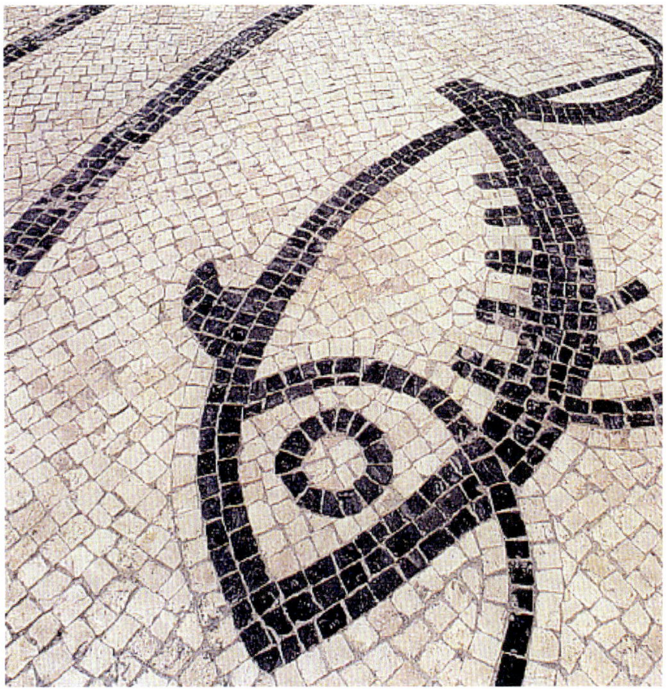

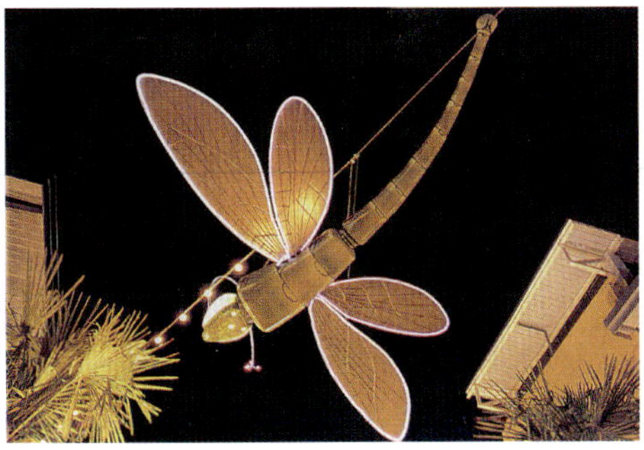

Project:
Salamanca Train Station

Location:	Salamanca, Spain
Owner/Developer:	Riofisa
	Salamanca, Spain
Designer/Architect:	Antonio Fernandez Alba
	Madrid, Spain
Gross Size of Center:	322,580 sq. ft.
Parking Spaces:	800
Opening Year:	March 2001

With an inventive approach to mixed-use, leisure and transportation, the center is wrapped around an existing train station to provide the city with an exciting new public space. The design balances the playful nature of the leisure and retail components with the institutional presence required by the rail authority. Salamanca stone projects a formal facade for the train station by day. At night, colorful lighting creates special effects that transform the center into a lively environment. The exterior plaza, a large public space for celebration, serves as a hinge between the day and night ambience and includes a tower that appears as a simple cone during the day, while changing colors create an eye-catching landmark for the city by night.

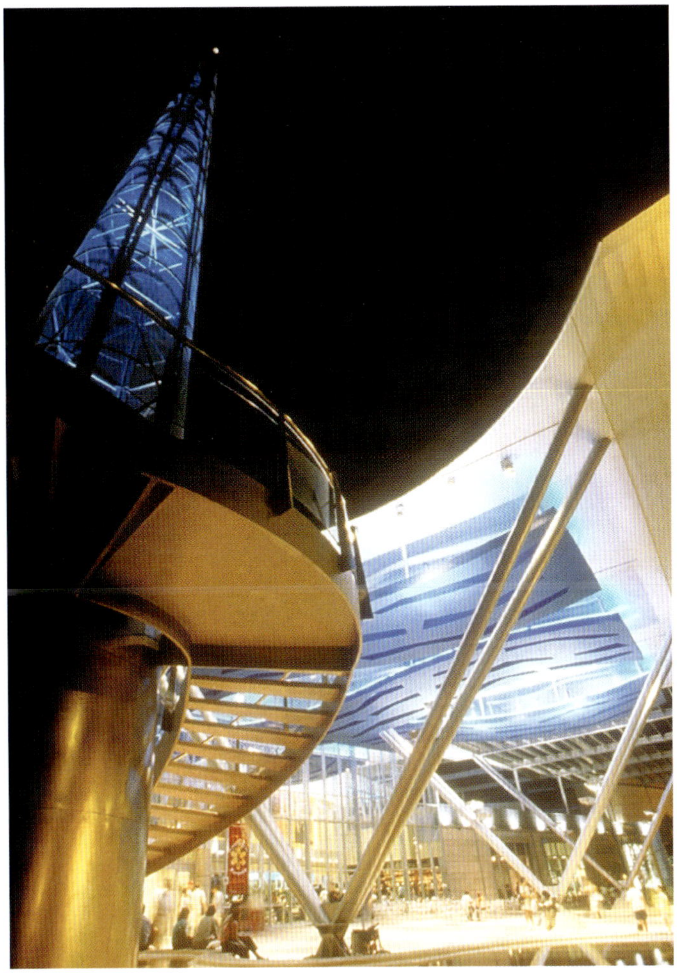

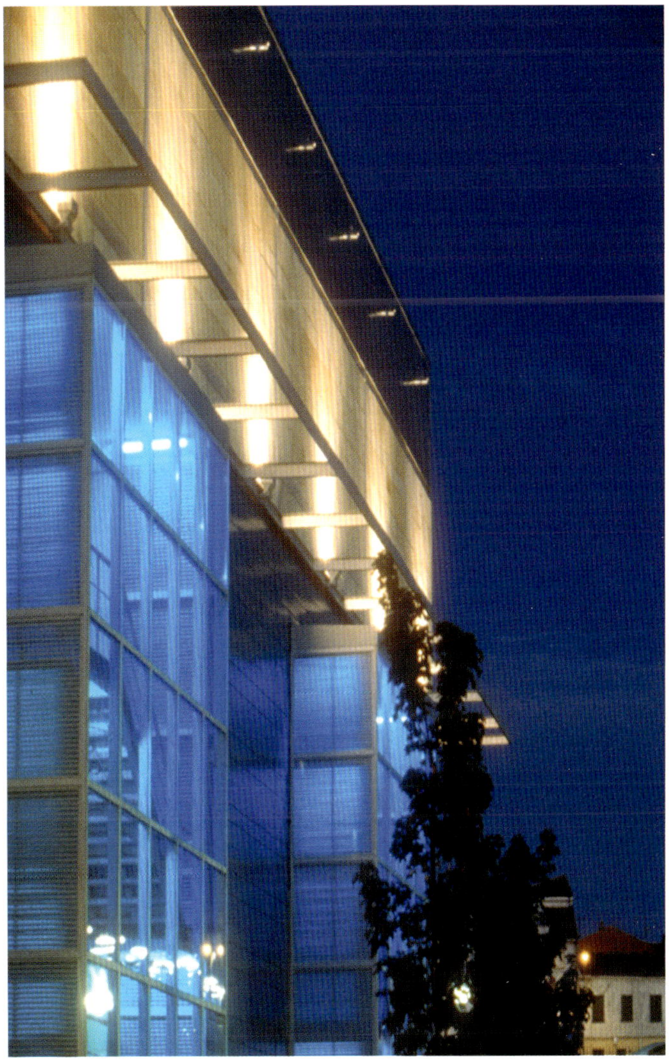

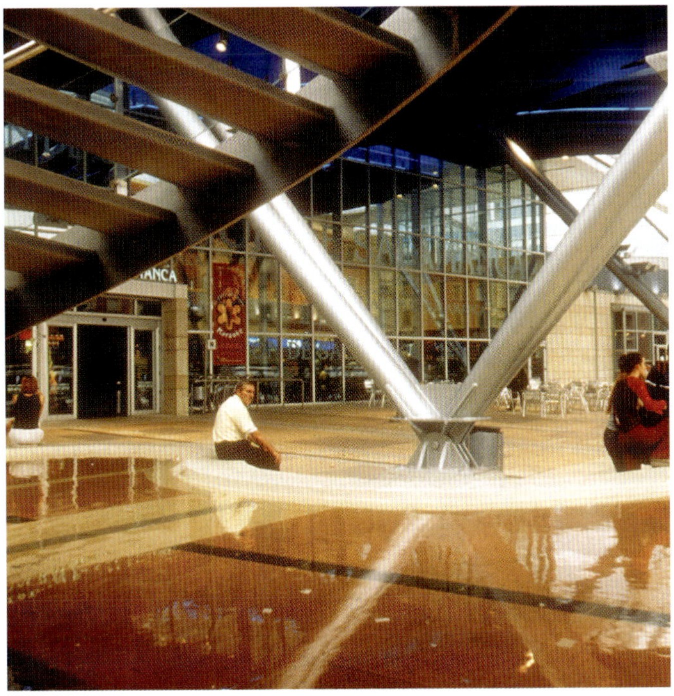

Project:
Val d' Europe

Location:	Marne-la-Vallée, France
Owner/Developer:	Secovalde Paris, France
Designer/Architect:	Graham Gund Architects Cambridge, Massachusetts, United States
Executive Architect:	5,200
Gross Size of Center:	957,640 sq. ft.
Parking Spaces:	5,200
Opening Year:	1998

The Val d' Europe is the keystone structure in the town of the same name, which is adjacent to Euro Disney. The architecture, an innovative, typically Parisian fusion of glass and metal, derives from the work of architects Haussman, Eiffel and Baltard. Comprised of a regional shopping center, a food court, a leisure area and outlets of top-quality international retailers, the complex plays on the beloved French icons of retail and leisure, including: Les Halles, an immense indoor market; Les Passages Parisiens, which owe their design to the famous Parisian shopping arcades; La Promenade, a thoroughfare of renovated facades punctuated by windows and covered by a glass roof; and Les Terrasses, a garden with cast-iron ornamentation that evokes the greenhouses of the 19th century.

79

Project:
Veso Mare

Location:	Patras, Greece
Owner/Developer:	Techno Ate
	Athens, Greece
Designer/Architect:	RTKL Associates, Inc., UK Ltd.
	London, United Kingdom
Executive Architect:	Archicon Ltd.
	Athens, Greece
Gross Size of Center:	322,920 sq. ft.
Parking Spaces:	500
Opening Year:	2001

Veso Mare borrows its name from the soap maker who was the original occupant of the site. Now, the historically listed warehouse buildings have been restored as part of the first leisure-only development in Greece. With its diverse assortment of entertainment, retail, restaurants and its most dynamic feature, public spaces that range from intimate corners for romantic meals to gathering places for large groups of friends, the development has become the heart of the community. Tourists arriving on ferries from Italy and other nearby areas are greeted by a large central plaza with an interactive water feature in an open-air setting that provides virtually no barrier between indoor and outdoor spaces. An amphitheater approach provides for multilevel stacking of retail, dining, entertainment and people-watching at every level—plus breathtaking views of the sea.

81

Project:
La Part-Dieu

Location:	Lyon, France
Owner/Developer:	Rodamco France, Paris, France
Designer/Architect:	BDP, London, England
Gross Size of Center:	1,082,580 sq. ft.
Parking Spaces:	4,200
Opening Year:	September 14, 2001 (Expansion)

A study of the characteristics of Lyon revealed three treasured traits: luminosity, as Lyon has a special quality of light; fluidity, as the city lies at the confluence of the Saône and Rhône rivers; and character, as seen in the high-quality building materials of the town. The renovation/expansion plan translated these traits into the design. Parts of the massive masonry of rooftop parking were cut away to allow for skylights that permit high levels of natural light as well as artificial light reflected off the brise-soleil. A reworked shopper-traffic system achieved a better flow of people—110,000 visitors on a typical Saturday. The character of the mall was enhanced through the use of sycamore-veneered panels; glass, steel and timber balustrades; new limestone and marble flooring and lighter finishes.

83

Project:
Almada Forum

Location:	Almada, Portugal
Owner/Developer:	Commerz Grundbesitz Investment-gesellschaft mbH Wiesbaden, Germany and Group Auchan Lisbon, Portugal
Designer/Architect:	T+T Design MC Gouda, The Netherlands
Gross Size of Center:	74,500 sq. ft.
Parking Spaces:	5,000
Opening Year:	September 18, 2002

Located at the intersection of two major highways and the main bridge over the Tagus River, Almada Forum is designed as an extension of the city. Unique architectural and pedestrian arcades present visitors with a constantly changing pattern of impressions and spaces similar to a traditional city center. The three main squares of the center include a Central Square that serves as a modern-day meeting place for community functions and exhibitions; a Western Square with a design based on earth and sun elements that is located in a naturally lit large glass dome with tropical waterfalls, large sculptured rocks and lush vegetation; and a Technological Court accented by a geometric high-tech decor. The food court is based on a typical local fishing village, acknowledging the region's cultural, nautical and maritime history.

85

Project: El Muelle Leisure and Shopping Centre

Location: Las Palmas de Gran Canaria, Las Palmas, Spain
Owner/Developer: Riofisa, S.A. Alcobendas, Madrid, Spain
Designer/Architect: Riofisa–Chapman Taylor Alcobendas, Madrid, Spain
Gross Size of Center: 682,571 sq. ft.
Parking Spaces: 1,300
Opening Year: April 11, 2003

El Muelle Leisure and Shopping Centre, situated on a unique site in the city of Las Palmas de Gran Canaria on Santa Catalina Dock next to the bus stations and inter-island ferry terminal, provides the perfect location in the city center. Conceived as a ship anchored in port, with stepped terraces that minimize its impact on the seafront, the seven-level shopping center uses high-quality materials that resist marine abrasion. A landscape of lakes, carefully planted vegetation and cybernetic fountains combined with large-format sculpture creates a sophisticated environment. Color and illumination suggest different impressions throughout the day as the facades of the cinemas reflect the gray sky of Las Palmas in the afternoon. Lighthouse towers and terraces are landmarks of the city skyline at night.

87

Project:
Altmarkt-Galerie Dresden

Location:	Dresden, Germany
Owner/Developer:	Altmarkt-Galerie Dresden KG Dresden, Germany
Designer/Architect:	Jost Hering; Hans Martin Hoffman Hamburg, Germany In cooperation with Prof. Dip.I-Ing. Manfred Schomers and Dipl.-Ing. Rainer Schürmann
Gross Size of Center:	279,864 sq. ft.
Parking Spaces:	520
Opening Year:	September 18, 2002

Sensitively integrated into historic Dresden, the Altmarkt-Galerie is a new-generation shopping center consisting of three three-level buildings adjacent to the city's main shopping area. Representative entry zones connect the new buildings with open space between the old and new buildings, which have been designed as high-class squares. The building design preserves a cellar vault from the 13th century, now occupied by a wine dealer. A sleek glass cube allows people to view the historic vault where findings from an archaeological excavation are exhibited. Within the center, an exhibit pays homage to the areas in the city that were destroyed in World War II and includes two models of Dresden—one prior to demolition and one modern.

89

Project:
Les Passages de l'Hôtel de Ville

Location:	Boulogne-Billancourt, France
Owner/Developer:	CECOBIL (AXA Reim France/ Klépierre) Paris, France
Designer/Architect:	Dusapin & Leclercq Paris, France
Gross Size of Center:	275,436 sq. ft.
Parking Spaces:	600
Opening Year:	May 31, 2004

Although Boulogne-Billancourt boasts an affluent population and is the largest city in the Ile de France after Paris, the urban fabric was a patchwork of interconnected, fiercely independent districts with a hodgepodge of run-down buildings that called for a town center. Les Passages updates the Parisian tradition of comfortable, busy arcades that blend with their surroundings with a series of covered streets that are a natural extension of the neighborhood. The center is easily accessible by public transport via two metro lines and eight bus lines. It can also be reached by car and on foot along the boulevard. An overhead canopy of clear glass allows the space to be filled with natural light. Shoppers walking to the center can see the building facades of the Grand'Place and Hôtel de Ville as the walkways of Les Passages become, in effect, Boulogne-Billancourt's town center.

91

Project:
Madrid Xanadú

Location:	Arroyomolinos, Madrid, Spain
Owner/Developer:	Madrid Xanadú 2003 S. L.
	Arroyomolinos, Madrid, Spain
Designer/Architect:	Chapman Taylor España
	Madrid, Spain
Gross Size of Center:	1,706,252 sq. ft.
Parking Spaces:	7,349
Opening Year:	May 16, 2003

Like Kublai Khan's Xanadu, the city of earthly delights, Madrid's Xanadú is a place for enjoyment. Artists and craftspeople from throughout Europe and the United States designed murals, furniture, custom chandeliers, sculpture and flooring to create an orchestrated composition of international art, fashion, textures and ornamentation inspired by regional Spanish imagery. The main streets and plazas are light-filled spaces with vaulted ceilings and bridges that span the openings between floors. Designed around a large, two-level elliptical space ringed with restaurants, bars, cafes and entertainment, the leisure center is a dynamic environment. On the upper level is La Terraza, where visitors dine under whimsical tree-inspired canopies as two large, rotating graphic disks and projection screens provide visual media messages. Parque de Nieve is the premiere entertainment venue, with a downhill ski slope that offers a year-round skiing experience.

93

Project:
Emmen Centre

Location:	Emmenbrücke, Switzerland
Owner/Developer:	Maus Frères SA, Geneva, Switzerland
Designer/Architect:	Haskoll, London, United Kingdom
Gross Size of Center:	457,470 sq. ft.
Parking Spaces:	2,400
Opening Year:	September 2002

The Emmen Centre in Switzerland, an early example of retail architecture designed by shopping center pioneer Victor Gruen, was recently revived to meet the changing demands of a new century's shoppers. The renovation included the addition of a new third floor, the remodeling of the department store, the creation of a food court and improvements to shopper traffic patterns and access. The introduction of new light sources, including new fixtures and a glazed roof light, was key to the transformation. Remodeled entrances and new signage bring the updated identity of the center directly to the street.

95

Project:
Bullring

Location:	Birmingham, United Kingdom
Owner/Developer:	The Birmingham Alliance Birmingham, United Kingdom
Designer/Architect:	Benoy London, United Kingdom
Gross Size of Center:	1,183,600 sq. ft.
Parking Spaces:	3,100
Opening Year:	September 4, 2003

Bullring is the scene of an architectural revolution that has collected the city's fragmented retail interests to return Birmingham's city center to its historic position as a market town, a distinction that dates from the 12th century. Although the entire project is newly built, it is knit into the existing fabric, grain and scale of the city. The project design embraces the city, yet the mixture of malls, open spaces, covered streets and open plazas feels fresh and inviting. Drawing on historic street patterns, Bullring links important thoroughfares and returns St. Martin's Church to its rightful public and emotional setting at the center of the project. Bullring marks a new era of retail-led regeneration for British cities. As one of the largest retail developments to be built in over a decade, Bullring is the first of its scale to be built in a city center.

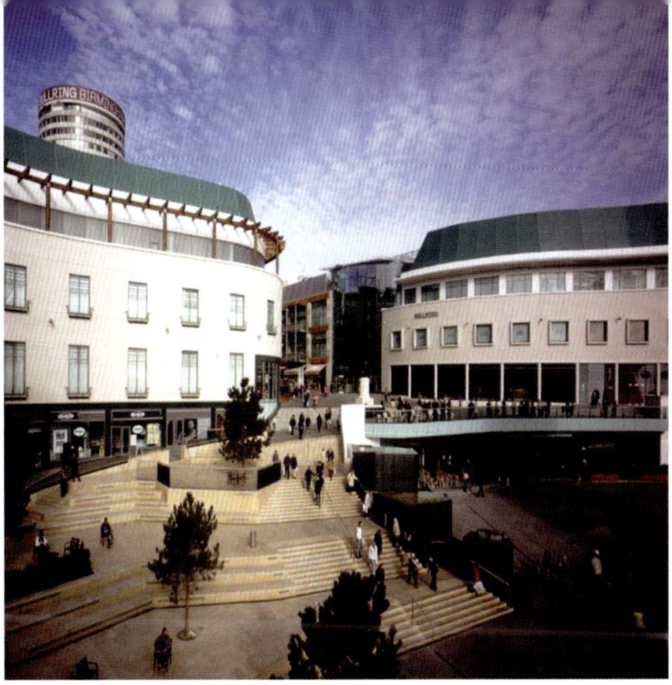

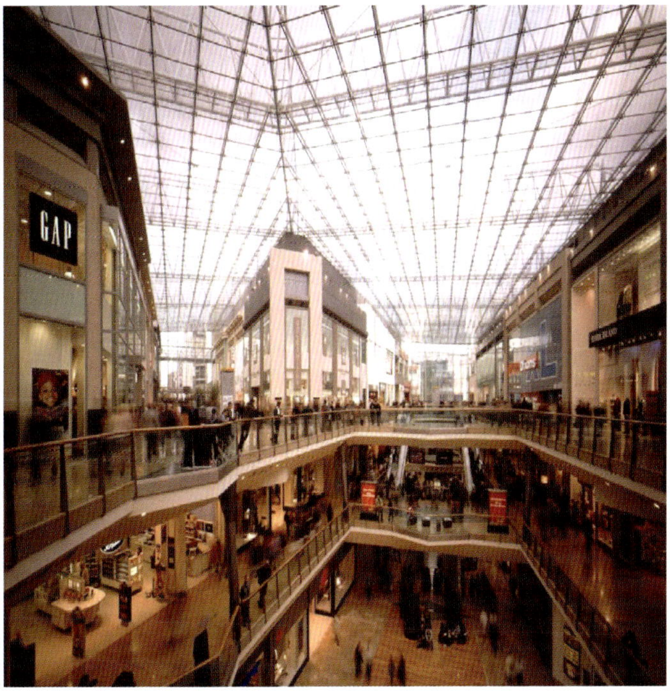
GAP

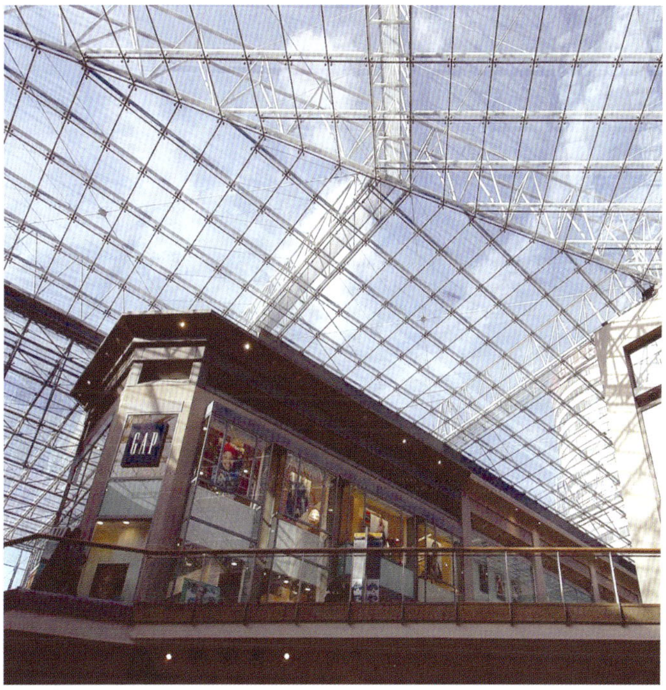
GAP

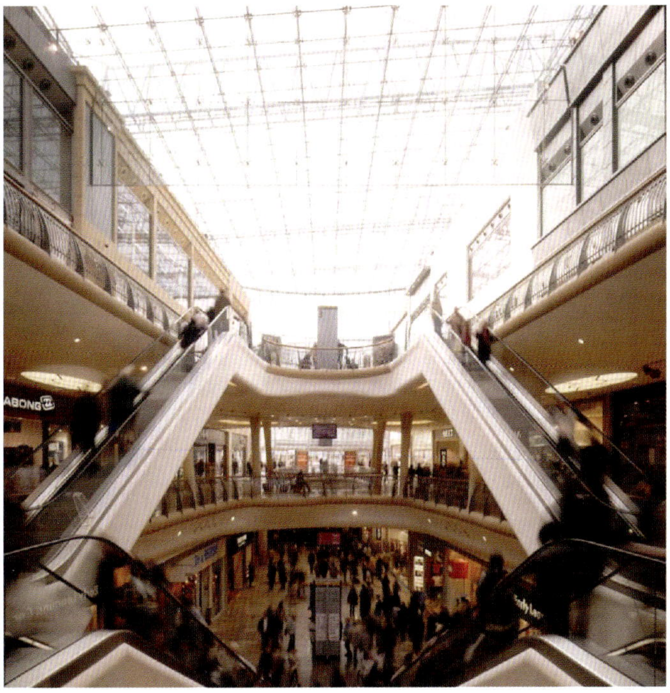

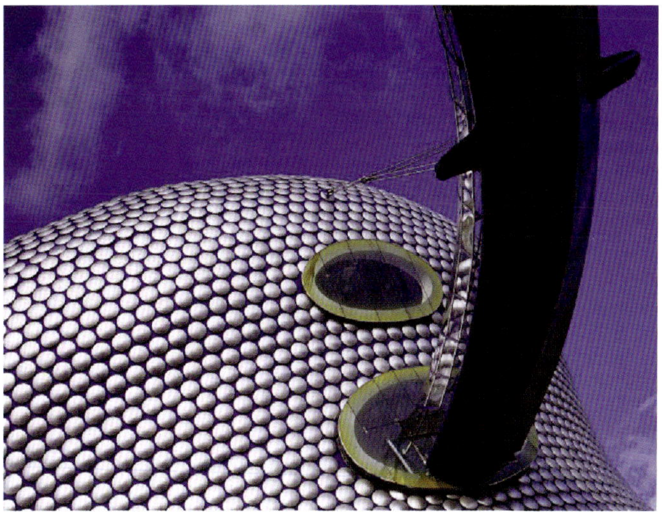

Project:
Estação Viana

Location: Viana do Castelo, Portugal
Owner/Developer: Sonae Sierra
Maia, Portugal
Designer/Architect: Laguarda.Low Architects
Dallas, Texas, United States
Gross Size of Center: 628,273 sq. ft.
Parking Spaces: 600
Opening Year: November 19, 2003

Estação Viana is located on a privileged site adjacent to the rail station in the center city of Viana do Castelo. The development has created a whole new dynamic for the city that capitalizes on its position at a transportation hub and offers a full array of shopping and leisure outlets in an attractive setting. The modern shopping center surrounds the railway tracks and incorporates the elements of the station—from its history to its shapes, sounds, smells and experiences—as inspiration for the design of the floors, the shelters, the graphics and even the display of the model train, which is suspended in front of a mural of the buildings and landscapes of Viana do Castelo. Estação Viana is also easily accessible to pedestrians and automobiles.

99

9. Latin America

Punta Langosta Cruise Terminal and Shopping Center
Cozumel, Quintana Roo, Mexico

Mall Plaza Norte
Santiago, RM, Chile

Terramall Shopping Center
San Jose, Costa Rica

Shopping Center Iguatemi Fortaleza
Fortaleza, Ceará, Brazil

Geographically Latin America stretches from the United States-Mexican border to the tip of Tierra del Fuego and includes 20 countries as well as several territories. While Portuguese is the official language of Brazil, the largest country in Latin America, Spanish is the principal language of the region. Among 20 countries there remain hundreds of cultural differences.

The distinctly vibrant and colorful traditions of each country continue to influence modern commercial environments. The influence of the European cultures that has been imported with waves of new settlers including the French, the Germans, the English, the Dutch, the Spanish and the Portuguese from the time of the conquests can be seen in the modern capitals, such as Mexico City, Rio de Janeiro, Buenos Aires and Santiago. Yet the native people retain many aspects of their own cultures in everything from the arts and music to the traditional markets.

Strong traditions of the *mercado*, the marketplace, infused with vibrant colors and rich textures bathed in filtered sunlight, create the cultural background against which new projects are compared. The visual density of products, balanced against ever-present sounds and fragrances, brings culture to the present day. Many newly constructed retail projects extend this legacy with contemporary interpretations.

Project: Punta Langosta Cruise Terminal and Shopping Center

Location:	Cozumel, Quintana Roo, Mexico
Owner/Developer:	GICSA
	Mexico, DF, Mexico
Designer/Architect:	GICSA Proyectos
	Mexico, DF, Mexico
Gross Size of Center:	95,764 sq. ft.
Opening Year:	January 2002

Punta Langosta on the island of Cozumel provides both the local inhabitants and the more than six million tourists who visit the island every year with a welcoming place of safe arrival as well as first-class shopping and recreation. With a restored lighthouse as its iconic image, the open-air shopping center skillfully adapts traditional Caribbean architecture to meet the modern needs of a cruise terminal. The design combines avant-garde design with novel elements such as a hanging bridge that connects the dock to the second floor and the incorporation of two canvas tensile structures that cover the common areas to protect shoppers from the intense sun.

103

Project:
Mall Plaza Norte

Location:	Santiago, RM, Chile
Owner/Developer:	Plaza Oeste S.A. (Mall Plaza)
	Santiago, RM, Chile
Designer/Architect:	TVS International
	Atlanta, Georgia, United States
Gross Size of Center:	1,829,865 sq. ft.
Parking Spaces:	2,284
Opening Year:	November 27, 2003

Mall Plaza Norte represents more to its community than just another regional mall, as it incorporates medical offices, big-box convenience retailers, cultural and performing arts venues and entertainment along with traditional fashion, food and specialty-store offerings that meet cultural and social needs. The design embraces the natural beauty of the surrounding environs, offering a variety of scenic views and capturing natural light that enlivens the interiors. Three department stores, a home center, a superstore, 120 small stores and an auto plaza comprise the mall, while the outdoor entertainment plaza creates a social destination for the entire community and includes restaurants, cinemas, a performing arts theater, a library and a branch of the National Museum of Art.

105

Project:
Terramall Shopping Center

Location:	San Jose, Costa Rica
Owner/Developer:	Grupo Bursatil Aldesa
	San Jose, Costa Rica
Designer/Architect:	Beame Architectural Partnership
	Coral Gables, Florida, United States
Executive Architect:	Ossenbach, Pendones & Bonilla
	San Jose, Costa Rica
Gross Size of Center:	501,213 sq. ft.
Parking Spaces:	1,200
Opening Year:	October 30, 2003

Nestled into the hillside of an existing coffee plantation with views of the spectacular Carpinteria Mountain, one of Costa Rica's most beautiful nature preserves, Terramall celebrates the environment. It is a thriving center that blends into the scenery to provide a dramatic view from the expressway, a pedestrian-scaled entry from local streets and a series of natural spatial environments that present the visitor with an opportunity for discovery. Through a series of forms that extend from the hillside, the mall becomes part of the landscape as the building profile slopes with the surrounding mountains and hills, reflecting the geometries of the spaces within, which are reinforced by the glow of the center's skylights. Retail shops and restaurants, sited to take advantage of the location, employ a simple and direct architecture to create dynamic spaces and highlight the views.

107

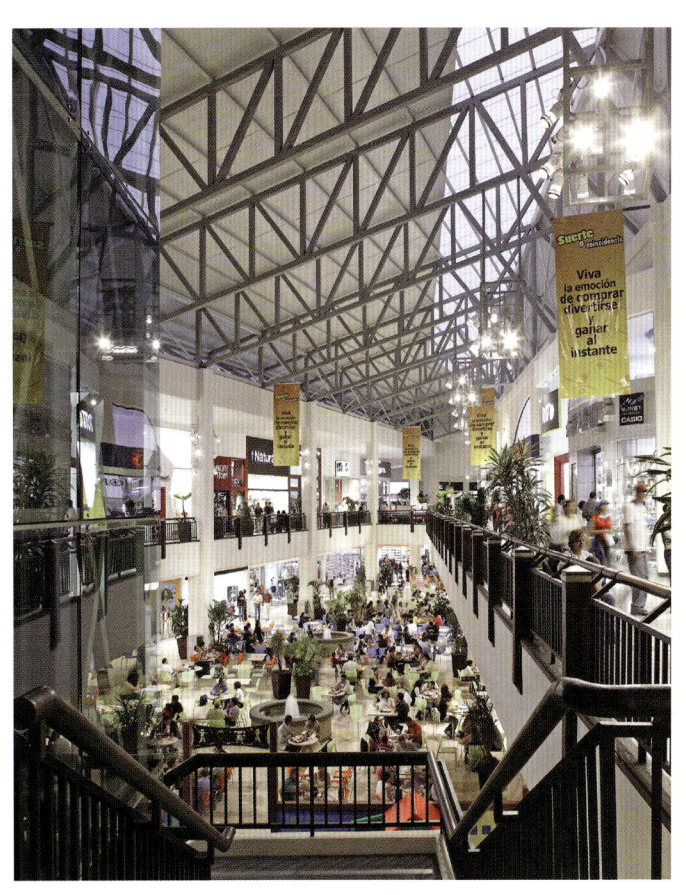

Project:
Shopping Center Iguatemi Fortaleza

Location:	Fortaleza, Ceará, Brazil
Owner/Developer:	Jereissati Centros Comerciais Fortaleza, Ceará, Brazil and Petros Fundacão Petrobras de Segridade Social Rio de Janeiro, Rio de Janeiro, Brazil
Designer/Architect:	ID8 Baltimore, Maryland, United States and RTKL Associates Inc. Dallas, Texas, United States
Gross Size of Center:	Before renovation/expansion: 467,34 sq. ft.; After renovation/expansion: 594,170 sq. ft.
Parking Spaces:	3,900 (500 added in renovation/ expansion)
Opening Year:	April 1982; Renovation/expansion: July 2003

The design concept behind the renovation and expansion of Shopping Center Iguatemi Fortaleza evokes the relationship of the people and the ocean as the city opens to the rest of the world. Developed on three levels and articulated around a central square, the project creates a playful atmosphere by mixing elements from local culture with modern materials and technologies as well as using stylized symbols such as the raft, fish, ocean waves and palm trees. Above the grand awning at the main entrance is a great kaleidoscope of mirrored glass. Shoppers are greeted by fountains, where water glides over sculpted glass walls with bas-reliefs of marine motifs and a granite floor of locally extracted granite arranged in regional themes. Adorning the bulkheads are inscriptions in a variety of languages, evoking concepts such as liberty, love and peace.

109

North America 10.

110
The Corner at Bellevue Square
Bellevue, Washington, United States

FlatIron Crossing
Broomfield, Colorado, United States

Mercado Plaza
Palm Springs, California, United States

The Grove
Los Angeles, California, United States

Desert Ridge Marketplace
Phoenix, Arizona, United States

Pentagon Row
Arlington, Virginia, United States

Birkdale Village
Huntersville, North Carolina, United States

The Mall at Millennia
Orlando, Florida, United States

The Market Common, Clarendon
Arlington, Virginia, United States

Dadeland Mall
Miami, Florida, United States

The Gardens on El Paseo
Palm Desert, California, United States

Fashion Show
Las Vegas, Nevada, United States

The Shops at Tanforan
San Bruno, California, United States

Victoria Gardens
Rancho Cucamonga, California, United States

The Streets at Southpoint
Durham, North Carolina, United States

La Encantada
Tucson, Arizona, United States

The Shops at Legacy
Plano, Texas, United States

Downtown Silver Spring
Silver Spring, Maryland, United States

The United States and Canada share more than a border—their early history and subsequent settlement patterns have created strong, multicultural societies marked by openness and innovation. Each country is also marked by regional differences that have as much to do with the climate and geography as with deep-rooted cultural traditions. As a result, North American retail centers are veritable breeding grounds for new formats and fresh ideas.

Retail history in the United States includes the high-style shopping streets lined with grand department stores, such as New York's Fifth Avenue and Chicago's Michigan Avenue, as well as small-town Main Streets where mom-and-pop shops shaped concepts of community. The suburban shopping mall was born here, too, giving several generations of shoppers convenience, access to national retailers and a gathering place.

Today a new generation of shoppers is returning to downtowns, where revitalized Main Streets with an improved mix of stores offer an alternative to the stand-alone mall. Developers and their designers are also creating new centers that give new meaning to the term "town center" because of their diverse scale, architectural style, stores, restaurants, entertainment venues and civic uses, including libraries and post offices.

The places of this visual tour are places made by not only their physical surroundings but also by their acceptance by the local and visiting communities, exhibiting that somehow they have stood the test of time. Consciously, they have made a place. Subconsciously, and more importantly, they have made place.

Project:
The Corner at Bellevue Square

Location:	Bellevue, Washington, United States
Owner/Developer:	F. Kemper Freeman, Jr.
	Bellevue, Washington, United States
Designer/Architect:	Sclater Partners Architects
	Seattle, Washington, United States
Gross Size of Center:	1,300,000 sq. ft.
Parking Spaces:	6,476
Opening Year:	1981; Expansion date: April 2001

The Corner at Bellevue Square is an infill, street-front retail project that responds to the new demand for pedestrian-oriented retail. The development was the catalyst for further street-oriented retail development of the downtown plan as downtown Bellevue became an urban epicenter of the area's high-tech community. Six unique building facades were created from materials such as brick, stone, wood, plaster and glass to meet the design goal of replicating the varied fabric of multiple buildings constructed at different times. A popular public gathering place is The Lodge—a 4,000-square-foot common area with a 40-foot-tall fireplace fashioned from stone with rustic steel grates, andirons, a heavy steel mantle, custom-made leather furniture and artfully designed coffee and sofa tables.

113

Project:
FlatIron Crossing

Location:	Broomfield, Colorado, United States
Owner/Developer:	Westcor Phoenix, Arizona, United States
Designer/Architect:	Callison Architecture, Inc. Seattle, Washington, United States
Gross Size of Center:	1,500,000 sq. ft.
Parking Spaces:	6,500
Opening Year:	August 2000

To garner customer loyalty and attract employees, the designers of FlatIron Crossing in the Denver suburb of Broomfield, Colorado, created a look and amenities consistent with the community's lifestyle, culture and environmental concerns. The enclosed mall, anchor tenants, a low-rise, open-air retail village and service and food outlets are arrayed in two sweeping curves. The entrance captures spectacular views of the Rocky Mountains and leads to a sequence of spaces, which include a sheltered meadow and pond, that end in a four-acre park with a waterfall, native vegetation, prairie views and a nearby trail system. The FlatIron Crossing Music and Art Foundation, the first nonprofit organization established by a regional shopping center to benefit a single cause on an ongoing basis, forges meaningful connections with the community.

115

Project:
Mercado Plaza

Location:	Palm Springs, California, United States
Owner/Developer:	Wessman Development Company, Palm Springs, California, United States
Designer/Architect:	Altevers Associates, San Diego, California, United States
Gross Size of Center:	7,603 sq. ft.
Parking Spaces:	150
Opening Year:	January 2000

Prior to the 1930s, the "Old Palm Springs" style of Mediterranean architecture was the hallmark of the city center. The redevelopment of Mercado Plaza revives the historic character of Palm Springs with a two-building, two-story retail/office complex separated by an inviting courtyard. The aesthetic aspects of the renovation include the use of stone columns, trellis-covered terraces, balconies, awnings, French doors that lead to terraces, twelve shades of lime-wash paint and custom wrought iron for railings and balconies. The revitalized center now fills the gap in the downtown pedestrian experience with its beautiful village-style courtyard that provides a gathering place for community socializing and expands the shopping experience.

117

Project:
The Grove

Location:	Los Angeles, California, United States
Owner/Developer:	Caruso Affiliated Holdings Santa Monica, California, United States
Designer/Architect:	Elkus/Manfredi Architects Ltd. Boston, Massachusetts, United States
Gross Size of Center:	575,000 sq. ft.
Parking Spaces:	3,504
Opening Year:	March 15, 2002

With world-renowned retail, dining and entertainment, The Grove is a major destination in Los Angeles and an integral part of the daily life of the local community. Set on 17.5 acres adjacent to the historic Farmers Market, The Grove evokes a visually rich, historic retail district, with a street that is anchored by the Farmers Market at one end and a town square at the other. An old-fashioned, double-deck trolley services the two landmarks by passing through connecting streets. The common areas are filled with landscaping, meandering walkways, wood benches and wrought iron tables. Two- and three-story buildings are highly articulated and inviting, offering varied storefronts, a format that has encouraged national tenants to establish unique flagship store prototypes. The town square embodies a quaint park that is lushly landscaped with a generous lawn, a lake with an arched pedestrian bridge over waterfalls and animated waters choreographed to music.

119

Project:
Desert Ridge Marketplace

Location:	Phoenix, Arizona, United States
Owner/Developer:	Vestar Development Co.
	Phoenix, Arizona, United States
Designer/Architect:	MCG Architecture
	Pasadena, California, United States
Gross Size of Center:	1,155,334 sq. ft.
Parking Spaces:	5,815
Opening Year:	November 2001

Desert Ridge Marketplace, a 1.2-million-square-foot open-air regional shopping, dining and entertainment experience, expands the concepts of regional malls, urban villages and lifestyle centers to create a unique "power village" with something for everyone. Five distinct shopping neighborhoods—hard goods, soft goods, neighborhood convenience, health and leisure, and lifestyle/entertainment/restaurants—are linked by lushly covered walkways and shaded promenades that provide an intimacy of scale. More than 80 percent of the native Sonoran Desert plant material located on-site was identified, preserved and replanted. Majestic rows of Canary Island Date Palms, desert willow trees, abundant bougainvilleas, pavers, torchéres and fountains create a sense of arrival. In contrast to the local flora, an area specifically for the Generation Y age group offers the latest high-energy videos on a massive 12-by-12-foot screen, a live performance stage and a rock-climbing wall.

121

Project:
Pentagon Row

Location:	Arlington, Virginia, United States
Owner/Developer:	Federal Realty Investment Trust Rockville, Maryland, United States
Designer/Architect:	RTKL Associates Washington, DC, United States
Gross Size of Center:	300,000 sq. ft.
Parking Spaces:	1,236
Opening Year:	March 2002

Pentagon Row, built on an 18-acre, high-traffic site that links Washington, DC, to the Virginia suburbs, serves a dense, affluent area that, until now, lacked a central gathering spot. Surrounded by 500 apartments and 300,000 square feet of retail space, the project's open plaza provides a community space for readings and concerts in the summer as well as a temporary ice rink in winter. Three stories of apartments cap two levels of community-based retail and cafes, a neighborhood grocery store, an international food market and a bevy of specialty restaurants. Lampposts, cafe seating, park benches and awnings contribute to a Main Street setting where a clock tower reminiscent of a traditional town center adds to the distinctive character.

123

Project:
Birkdale Village

Location:	Huntersville, North Carolina, United States
Owner/Developer:	The Inland Real Estate Group, Inc.
	Oak Brook, Illinois, United States
Designer/Architect:	Shook Kelley, Inc.
	Charlotte, North Carolina, United States
	and
	The Housing Studio
	Charlotte, North Carolina, United States
Gross Size of Center:	725,185 sq. ft.
Parking Spaces:	2,101
Opening Year:	September 2002

At the heart of a 52-acre, traditionally planned community with multiple housing choices, Birkdale Village offers varied lifestyle options for recreation, entertainment, shopping, leisure, dining and neighborhood services. Located near one of North Carolina's largest inland lakes, the project is loosely patterned after New England seacoast towns. With its thoughtful urban plan and craftlike details, the multiuse project has become the new downtown for a bedroom community that had no traditional center. Not only does it provide public spaces and retail for neighborhoods that are within walking distance, its smart-growth approach contributes to the economic health of the region. As a result, this pedestrian-oriented development is a highly popular regional destination as well as home to hundreds of people.

125

Project:
The Mall at Millennia

Location:	Orlando, Florida, United States
Owner/Developer:	The Forbes Company
	Southfield, Michigan, United States
	and
	Taubman Centers, Inc.
	Bloomfield Hills, Michigan, United States
Designer / Architect:	JPRA Architects
	Farmington Hills, Michigan, United States
Gross Size of Center:	1,118,000 sq. ft.
Parking Spaces:	5,430
Opening Year:	October 18, 2002

Designed in an international contemporary style that is more civic than commercial, The Mall at Millennia provides the Orlando metropolitan area with a friendly place for people of all ages and gender. Geometric forms of circles, squares and triangles in exposed stainless steel, glass, stone and wood become the architectural envelopes and interiors. The unique S-shaped plan allows for a variety of tenant depths, while still maintaining the rectangular shape. Monumental entrances at all levels include: a Water Garden entry, with a "universe, earth and time" theme that includes programmed lighting and fountain features; an upper-level Winter Garden, which has a glass lobby with an orange orchard of whimsical garden life; and a Grand Court, which includes a circular group of 35-foot-high masts that identify the 12 calendar months, with a poetic narrative etched in glass.

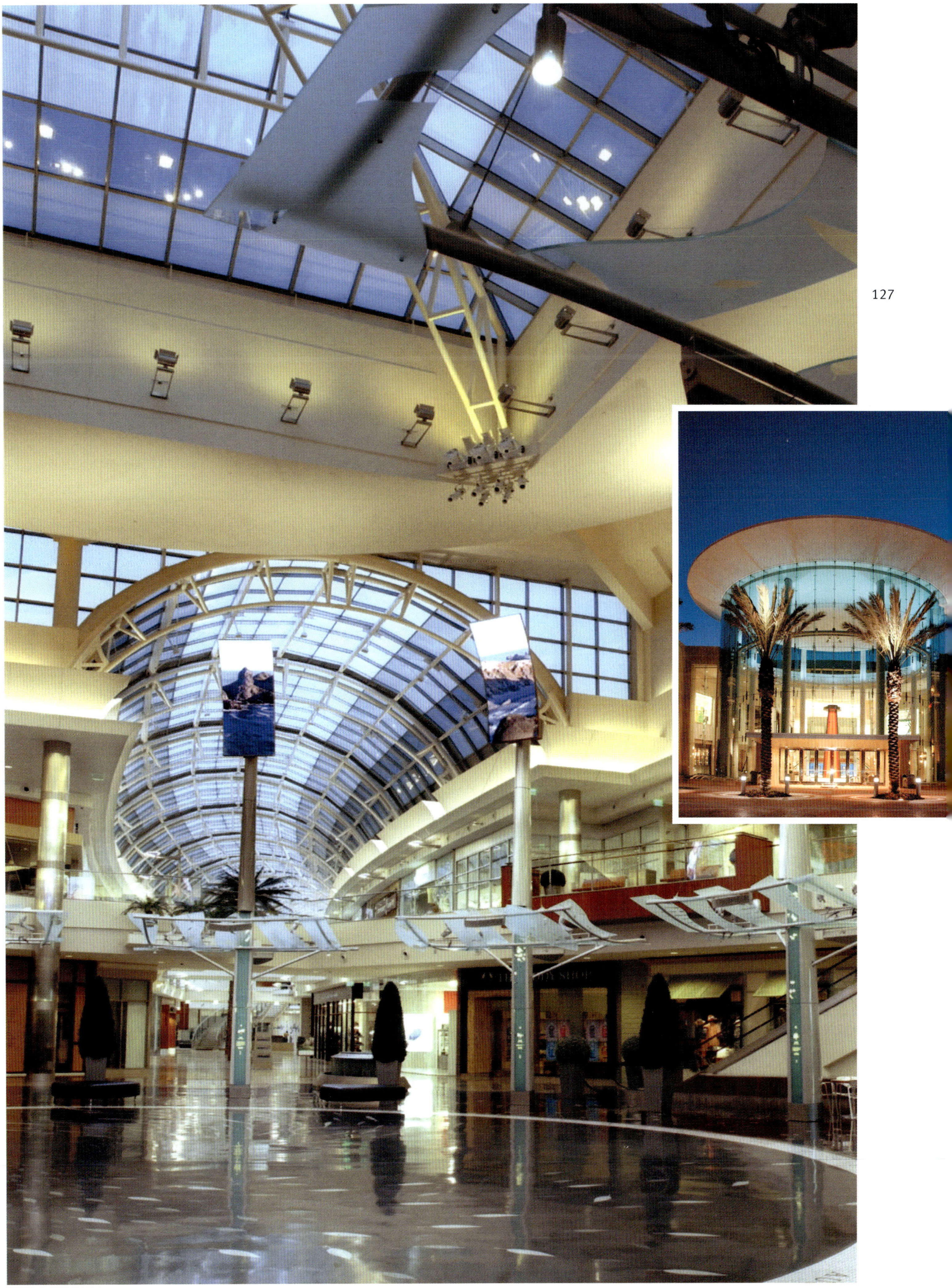

Project:
The Market Common, Clarendon

Location:	Arlington, Virginia, United States
Owner/Developer:	Clarendon Edgewood 10, LLC; CoPERA, RREEF, McCaffery Interests
	Chicago, Illinois, United States
Designer/Architect:	Antunovich Associates
	Chicago, Illinois, United States
Gross Size of Center:	1,232,181 sq. ft.
Parking Spaces:	1,310
Opening Year:	November 2001 (Phase I) and November 2003 (Phases II and III)

The Market Common, a town center for the Clarendon neighborhood, has become the catalyst for a rebirth spurring $1 billion in new development in the immediate neighborhood. A mixed-use development located along the Roslyn-Ballston Metrorail corridor in Arlington, Virginia, and immediately adjacent to Washington, D.C., the property is surrounded by single-family-home neighborhoods and comprises offices, retail, restaurants, for-lease housing, for-sale housing, parking and open park lands. The Market Common is the central meeting place that has a small-town feel, with stores and restaurants surrounding a central courtyard along with water fountains, public art and a children's play area. An internal street connects the courtyard with Clarendon Boulevard and provides 34 on-street parking spaces for retail and restaurant patrons.

129

Project:
Dadeland Mall

Location:	Miami, Florida, United States
Owner/Developer:	Simon Property Group
	Indianapolis, Indiana, United States
	and
	Morgan Stanley's Prime Property Fund
	Atlanta, Georgia, United States
Designer/Architect:	Thompson, Ventulett, Stainback & Associates
	Atlanta, Georgia, United States
Gross Size of Center:	1,310,000 sq. ft.
Parking Spaces:	6,879 (300 parking spaces added in renovation)
Opening Year:	1962; Expansion date: April 2003

"The place that has brought you the art of fashion for over 40 years has become a work of art itself." That tagline aptly describes the renovation of Miami's long-dominant mall, which was much in need of a cohesive design and an updated image and amenities. Catering to the local, multicultural customers as well as tourists whose tastes range from sophisticated to edgy, the new design incorporates forms inspired by the clean geometries of South Beach, the glamour of Miami and the lush Florida landscape, with its sun and shadow and soft beach colors. A "jewel box" entrance creates an iconic identity, while the entrance lobby welcomes customers. During the day, shadows softly wash across the space. At night, the space is dramatically illuminated. A cabana atmosphere enlivens the food court, where details such as embossed geckos play on the columns and the backlit art glass.

131

Project:
The Gardens on El Paseo

Location: Palm Desert, California, United States
Owner/Developer: Madison Realty Partnership
Designer/Architect: Altoon + Porter Architects, LLP
Los Angeles, California, United States
Gross Size of Center: 209,000 sq. ft.
Parking Spaces: 1,000
Opening Year: Fall 1999

The contemporary retail facilities and pedestrian amenities at The Gardens on El Paseo have become an architectural landmark in Palm Desert's premier shopping district. The Gardens is a two-level mall along the street El Paseo that embraces the pedestrian activity along the commercial corridor. A main entrance marked by a sculpture welcomes shoppers. Designed as simple forms with refined detailing, the buildings use indigenous materials and rich earth colors that resonate with the environment. The centerpiece of the complex is a richly landscaped plaza where delicate trellis structures are interspersed with the more solid building forms to create a quiet sense of formal order. In spite of the sometimes-harsh desert climate, The Gardens on El Paseo provides a comfortable shopping environment with the astute use of traditional forms and climate control.

133

Project:
Fashion Show

Location:	Las Vegas, Nevada, United States
Owner/Developer:	The Rouse Company Columbia, Maryland, United States
Designer/Architect:	Altoon + Porter Architects, LLP Los Angeles, California, United States
Conceptual Design:	Richard Orne, AIA, Orne & Associates and Laurin B. Askew, Jr., FAIA, Monk LLC
Design Manager for The Rouse Company:	Richard Orne, AIA, Orne & Associates
Gross Size of Center:	1,768,150 sq. ft.
Parking Spaces:	4,800
Opening Year:	1981; Renovation: 2003

The redevelopment of Fashion Show not only doubled the size of the already one-million-square-foot project, it repositioned the center to capitalize on the evolving pedestrian nature of the Las Vegas Strip. While the design takes its cue from the name and content of the Fashion Show, it is the antithesis of the themed hotels and casinos nearby. The center establishes its presence with a large high-tech structure known as The Cloud, which is suspended 180 feet in the air above a 72,000-square-foot plaza just off of Las Vegas Boulevard. The Cloud provides visual entertainment, shade for shoppers and passersby and an iconic image for the mall. Beneath the structure, a sophisticated audiovisual system projects images to and from the plaza and The Cloud with a series of supersized LED screens. With 1,000 feet of street frontage, the center attracts a growing share of local shoppers and the tourist market, especially international visitors.

135

Project:
The Shops at Tanforan

Location:	San Bruno, California, United States
Owner/Developer:	Wattson-Breevast
	Newport Beach, California, United States
Designer/Architect:	Altoon + Porter Architects, LLP
	Los Angeles, California, United States
Gross Size of Center:	1,041,000 sq. ft.
Parking Spaces:	4,570
Opening Year:	1971; Renovation: October 2005

The recently transformed Shops at Tanforan creates a large, transit-oriented, mixed-use commercial center in keeping with the changing context of the region. An expanded tenant program brings a multiscreen cinema and additional shopping and restaurants to the center. A new entry plaza with restaurants, cafes, a bookstore, outdoor dining and a playful water feature create a relationship with the street. Inside, the redesigned concourses and center court create a civic space that connects to the BART station. Future expansion plans make provisions for the addition of a new department store, new inline shops and a new parking structure. Moreover, the entire project was designed with a sustainable approach that makes the center a good neighbor in multiple ways that will continue to benefit the community over time.

137

Project:
Victoria Gardens

Location:	Rancho Cucamonga, California, United States
Owner/Developer:	Forest City Enterprises Los Angeles, California, United States and Lewis Investment Company Upland California, California, United States
Design Architects:	Altoon + Porter Architects, LLP Los Angeles, California, United States and Field Paoli San Francisco, California, United States and Elkus Manfredi Architects Boston, Massachusetts, United States
Gross Size of Center:	1,400,000 sq. ft.
Parking Spaces:	6,700
Opening Year:	October 2004

The design for Victoria Gardens draws in elements common to all towns as well as the special qualities of the singular place. Built on a classic street grid, the project incorporates a town square, courtyards, paseos, pocket parks and plazas. The individuality of the shops and buildings, designed by teams from several architectural firms, creates the sense of a town that reflects the values of a multigenerational community. Two-story retail shops, second- and third-floor office space and residential lofts above stores define a city-like scale. Civic spaces, including a children's performing theater, a conference center and a central library, are placed around a civic square, bringing an institutional component to the community. The landscape and urbanscape elements add distinction and differentiation.

139

Project:
The Streets at Southpoint

Location:	Durham, North Carolina, United States
Owner/Developer:	The Rouse Company
	Columbia, Maryland, United States
Designer/Architect:	RTKL Architects
	Baltimore, Maryland, United States
Gross Size of Center:	1,300,000 sq.ft.
Parking Spaces:	6,544
Opening Year:	March 8, 2002

At The Streets at Southpoint, in the historic Southern city of Durham, North Carolina, design features echo the town's traditional roots, such as a two-story brick warehouse structure that emulates stately downtown tobacco buildings. The 1.3-million-square-foot development creates a traditional townscape complete with individualized store "buildings," outdoor dining, shopping and entertainment areas in addition to an enclosed two-level regional mall. The distinction between interior and exterior shopping streets is deliberately blurred with the use of a sheer glass facade. Details such as architectural paving, lighting and sculptural features contribute to the fresh Main Street-inspired shopping experience.

141

Project:
La Encantada

Location:	Tucson, Arizona, United States
Owner/Developer:	Westcor Partners Phoenix, Arizona, United States
Designer/Architect:	Callison Architecture, Inc. Seattle, Washington, United States
Gross Size of Center:	269,468 sq. ft.
Parking Spaces:	1,600
Opening Year:	March 2004

An upscale specialty center in the heart of Tucson, La Encantada is a two-level, open-air lifestyle center inspired by the distinctive culture of the Southwest. Boasting the attributes and amenities of a resort, the center features plazas designed for entertainment and community events, landscaping with native plants and architecture that evokes the region to create a retail experience unique to the Tucson community. The architecture draws on the traditions of the city, while the designs work with, rather than against, the desert environment as shops circle the courtyards, breezeways and patios. Varied architectural references provide a sense of history, while a muted palette of sand, sage and putty blends with the setting, and materials and environmental graphics emphasize Southwestern arts and crafts.

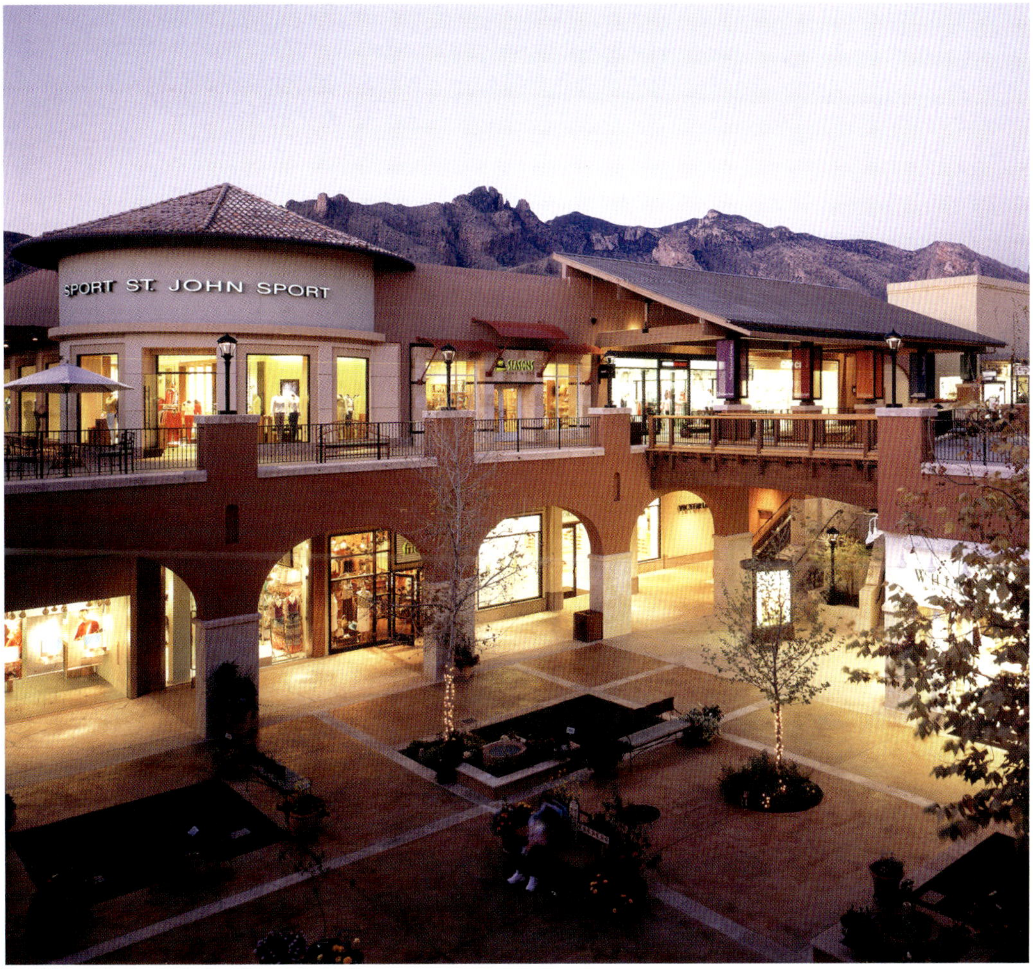

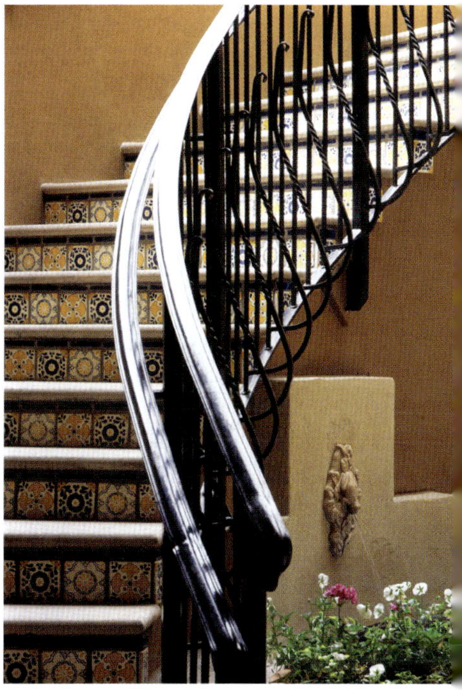

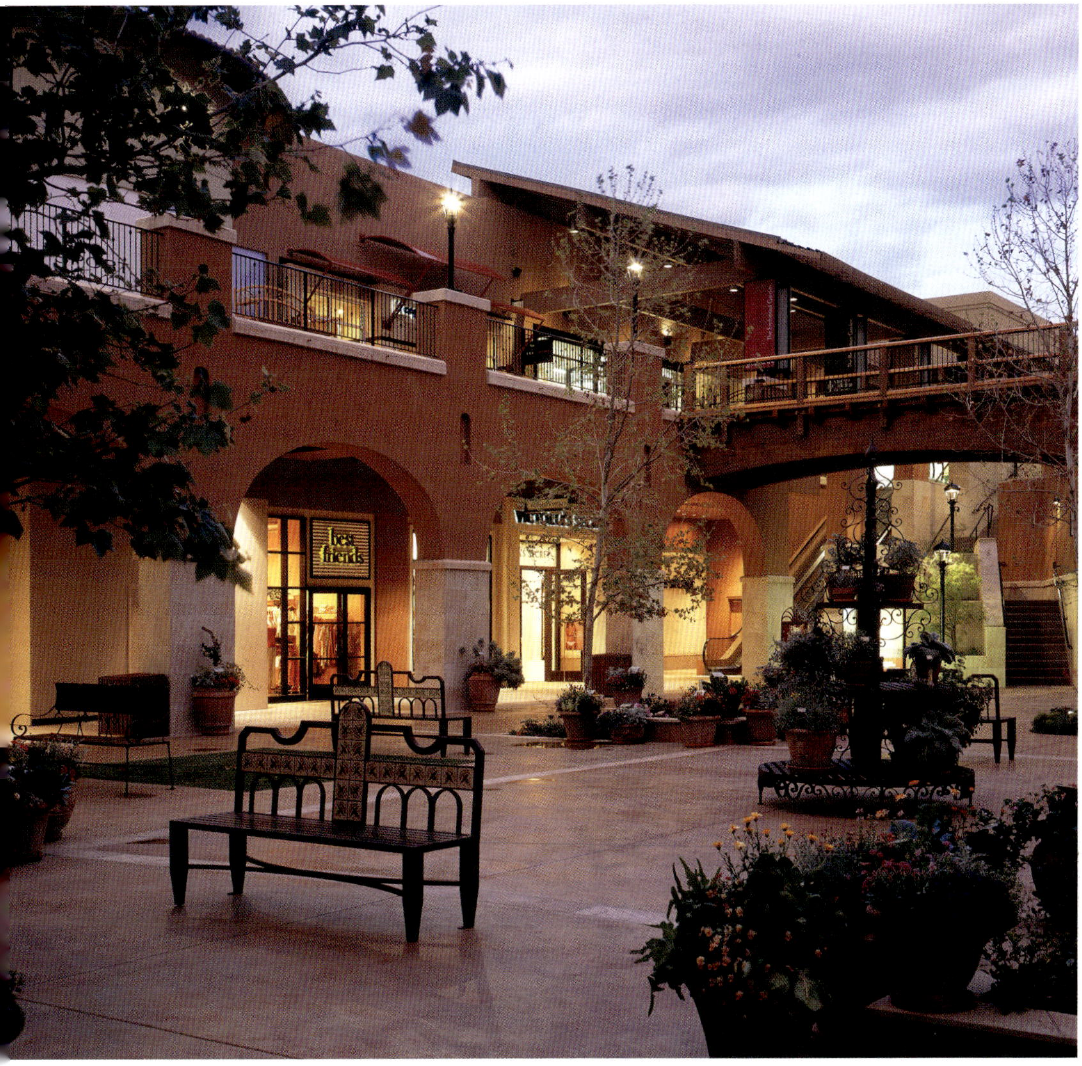

Project:
The Shops at Legacy

Location:	Plano, Texas, United States
Owner/Developer:	The Shops at Legacy L.P.
	Plano, Texas, United States
Designer/Architect:	RTKL Associates Inc.
	Dallas, Texas, United States
Gross Size of Center:	315,000 sq. ft.
Parking Spaces:	1,366
Opening Year	June 23, 2004

As part of a 150-acre master plan that transformed an empty plot in Plano, Texas, into a dynamic mixed-use environment, The Shops at Legacy serves as the town center's commercial spine, providing a holistic streetscape environment that is a rare discovery in the suburban sprawl that characterizes North Dallas. An eclectic mix of retail, restaurants and entertainment uses are integrated with upper-level office space that offers an essential Main Street sensibility. On-street parking enhances a pedestrian-oriented layout and serves as a traffic buffer. Sidewalks culminate in a lakefront park that provides access to a Marriott Hotel and an adjacent corporate campus. The development offers a sustainable, mixed-use alternative to the nearby regional malls, attracting shoppers with a street ambience and an inviting park and public spaces—all in a pedestrian-friendly environment that is hard to find in the region.

145

Project:
Downtown Silver Spring

Location:	Silver Spring, Maryland, United States
Owner/Developer:	PFA (a joint venture between The Peterson Companies, Foulger-Pratt Companies and Argo Investments)
	Silver Spring, Maryland, United States
Designer/Architect:	RTKL Associates Inc.
	Baltimore, Maryland, United States
Gross Size of Center:	265,000 sq. ft.
Parking Spaces:	3,112 spaces
Opening Year:	1938; Renovation: 2004

Redevelopment and new construction at Downtown Silver Spring transformed a historic site that had been vacant for 10 years into a vibrant, mixed-use retail and entertainment venue. Hailed as the catalyst for the revitalization of the neighborhood, the project achieved an amazing 180-degree turnaround on a vacant, crime-ridden eyesore. With the historic 1938 35,000-square-feet Silver Spring Shopping Center and Silver Theater as the initial building blocks, the development, which the city of Silver Spring fought hard to make happen, created the opportunity for a high-quality urban streetscape. The architecture of the new buildings is compatible with, but does not replicate, the existing Art Deco structures. A centrally located, interactive fountain acts as a giant watercooler for visitors as the Silver Plaza fills up with a diverse group of residents from throughout the region.

147

11: The Pacific

Queen Ka'ahumanu Center
Kahului, Maui, Hawaii, United States

Ala Moana Center
Honolulu, Hawaii, United States

2100 Kalakaua Avenue
Honolulu, Hawaii, United States

Waikiki Beach Walk
Honolulu, Hawaii, United States

THE PACIFIC ISLANDS, ALSO called Oceania, consists of tens of thousands of islands and usually includes New Zealand as well as the islands of Melanesia, Micronesia and Polynesia. For the purpose of this book, New Zealand has been grouped with its neighbor Australia, with whom it shares many cultural characteristics.

In spite of our picture-postcard images of the land and the climate, there are differences. Many islands, especially in Polynesia, have sparkling white beaches, palm trees and ocean breezes. Yet there are mountain peaks, volcanoes and steamy jungles, too.

Culturally, the Pacific Islands host two different ways of life. Traditional island culture continues as it has for centuries, with islanders living in small villages and supporting themselves by farming and fishing. However, when the Europeans arrived in the 1500s, they brought their own ways, and the cultural importation remains a strong force. Busy cities and popular tourist destinations are fully Westernized, offering sophisticated architecture and the best hotels and shops.

This is especially true in Hawaii, where native Polynesian traditions exist alongside the American influences as well as those of the many Asians who have long been residents of the Hawaiian islands. The result is a vibrant cultural mix that supports a variety of retail forms. The social and cultural patterns that are part of the relaxed island lifestyle are expressed in retail designs that are less formal. The best of these centers also take advantage of the beautiful setting and benign climate with shopping environments designed to meet the needs of the local residents and, perhaps more importantly, those of the many tourists who visit year-round.

Project:
Queen Ka'ahumanu Center

Location:	Kahului, Maui, Hawaii, United States
Owner/Developer:	Maui Land and Pineapple Company, Inc.
	Kahului, Maui, Hawaii, United States
Designer/Architect:	Altoon + Porter Architects, LLP
	Los Angeles, California, United States
Gross Size of Center:	272,866 sq. ft.
Parking Spaces:	2,880
Opening Year:	Summer 1994

Queen Ka'ahumanu Center is an architectural landmark with a contemporary identity that embraces the island's unique climate and character. A skylight connects the interior with the island's natural environment to provide views of the sky and the mountains. A translucent fabric skylight crown that spans the public space alludes to the billowing sails of tall ships that first brought trade to the Hawaiian islands. The design helps to conserve energy, provide ample daylight and dissipate heat buildup by shielding the indoor spaces from ultraviolet rays.

Graphics pay homage to the island heritage with a regal profile of Queen Ka'ahumanu, the project's namesake, wearing a festive wedding lei, while others are based on local flora. Paving patterns reflect the play of light on the ocean's surface and coral reefs, while custom fixtures evoke native torchlights.

151

Project:
Ala Moana Center

Location:	Honolulu, Hawaii, United States
Owner/Developer:	General Growth Properties Ala Moana LLC
	Honolulu, Hawaii, United States
Designer/Architect:	Callison Architecture, Inc.
	Seattle, Washington, United States
Gross Size of Center:	1,800,000 sq. ft.
Parking Spaces:	8,980
Opening Year:	1959; Renovation: Spring 1999

The renovation and expansion of the Ala Moana Center is unique to Hawaii in that it pays tribute to the spirit, tradition, culture and environment of Hawaii. These elements draw the locals as well as visitors to the center. The architecture serves as a framework and backdrop to the retail and entertainment activities. The inherent qualities of Ala Moana were heightened by the center's position as a tropical open-air center with a presence along the beach and mountain edges. The visitor is meant to experience the landscape of the island, from mountain to ocean. The design allows for opportunities to enjoy the sunshine, fresh breezes and beautiful vistas, with provisions along the way for areas of respite. Locals have embraced Ala Moana and see it as an important component of their community.

153

Project:
2100 Kalakaua Avenue

Location: Honolulu, Hawaii, United States
Owner/Developer: Honu Group, Inc.
Honolulu, Hawaii, United States
Designer/Architect: eight inc.
Honolulu, Hawaii, United States
Gross Size of Center: 111,000 sq. ft.
Opening Year: November 2002

This 111,000-square-foot retail complex is as much an urban idea as an architectural response. The design is the basis for a new Waikiki experience. The concept places an emphasis on graciousness reminiscent of old Hawaii. It draws on the natural assets of the area, its environment, local culture, institutions, characters and events. This idea is reflected in individually articulated storefronts. Each store heightens the retail expectations of the area with architecture made of refined proportions and sensitively scaled materials. Stone is the dominant material, and it gracefully illustrates the passage of time and symbolizes endurance.

155

Project:
Waikiki Beach Walk

Location:	Honolulu, Hawaii, United States
Owner/Developer:	Outrigger Enterprises Group
	Honolulu, Hawaii, United States
Designer/Architect:	Altoon + Porter Architects, LLP
	Los Angeles, California, United States
Gross Size of Center:	90,000 sq. ft.
Parking Spaces:	284
Opening Year:	May 2007

Outrigger, the owner of a number of the most popular tourist hotels, created this must-see destination on Lewers Street that celebrates the heritage of Hawaii. The triangle formed by Kalakaua and Lewers streets and the beachfront draws thousands of visitors daily and is a perfect setting for Waikiki Beach Walk. Fanciful fabric waves create an iconic gateway to the district that features the Hawaiian Walk of Fame and the Avenue of the Fountains, which recalls the island's sacred stream.

157

The Language of Enclosed Shopping Centers

International Shopping Center Architecture: Details, Concepts & Projects, published by ICSC in 1996, introduced the basic elements or language of shopping centers—the Nouns, Verbs, Adverbs and Adjectives—that are common to all retail buildings, regardless of locale, crossing all national borders. An analysis of the language of enclosed regional malls for the most part, it demonstrated how these elements, taken together, created a sentence structure that allowed for the distinct narratives. We reprise the concepts, as these elements remain essential to the design of the enclosed mall.

Details That Travel Well

Although overall shopping center concepts may not travel well, many of their programmatic elements and details do. These pieces are the "nouns, adjectives and verbs" of the "language" of the regional shopping center. Broken apart and reassembled, they apply to new concepts that transcend borders.

Entrances

Retail centers contain enormous human energy. If the eyes are the windows to the soul, so the entrances of a center become reflections of its energy. Beyond being the first and last impression of the shopping center experience, entrance elements reflect the interior architecture and convey the quality of the building and the merchants to the customer outside. They function as a logo identity of the shopping center. Where there are chauffeured vehicles or public transit, entrances serve as the foyer designed to handle larger numbers of people.

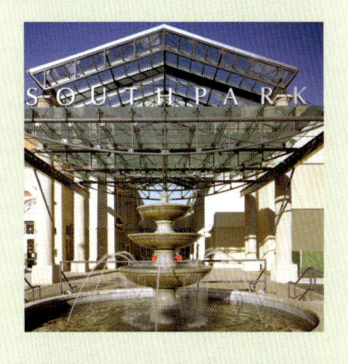

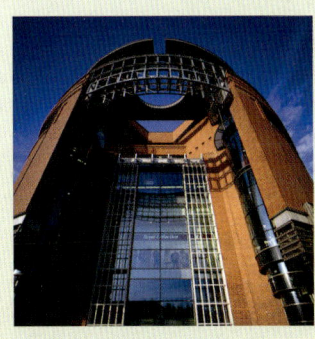

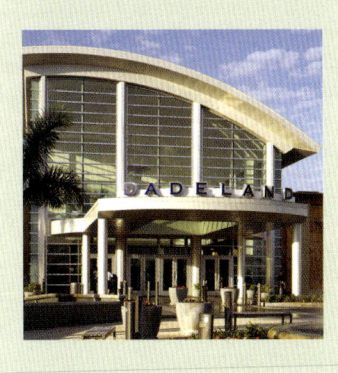

Paving

Paving is an element that every customer touches. As the most visible and memorable surface, it represents the greatest opportunity for an owner to convey quality. More than the critical issues of maintenance and performance need to be addressed in selecting the surfaces: the paved area establishes the overall ambience of a shopping center. The opportunities for contextual and cultural individuality are endless, as this element defines the character of the shopping experience.

161

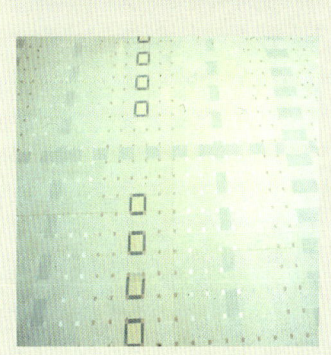

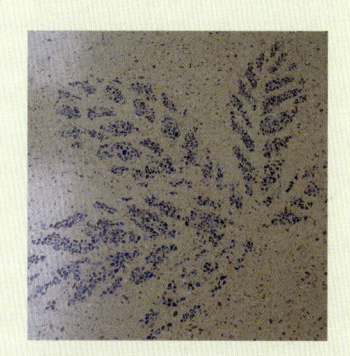

Handrails

Apart from providing physical protection and security, the hand- rail, like a ribbon of light, reflects the quality of a center through its design refinement, transparency and cleanliness. Elements that customers touch convey small tactile messages that reinforce the larger concept of quality. Visibility of shops on upper levels is facilitated or encumbered by the design of the handrail.

Stairs

Climbing through space requires human energy, yet it needs not be a chore. Stairs designed to feel like a grand place of arrival orient the customer to other destinations within a center. Utilitarian stairs denote work—something the shopper resents. Stairs designed to engage the customer contribute positively to the overall experience.

Escalators

These "staircases" moving through space must reinforce the overall customer circulation plan for a shopping center. Properly situated, they work in concert with the merchandising plan. With a captive rider, they present extraordinary opportunities for promotional displays and activities. Wider treads help make escalators more user-friendly, especially to shoppers with young children or the elderly.

Elevators

Glass-enclosed, oversized elevators are user-friendly, allowing patrons with baby carriages or disabilities easy access to a center. Often designed as colorful, decoratively lit, playful objects, elevators have become places from which and in which to promote the excitement of a center. Elevators, when utilized as an experience as well as a convenience, are a dynamic element that provide a visual draw to all levels they serve.

Balconies

Like opera boxes at La Scala, the famous opera house in Milan, Italy, balconies add a level of interest to the overall center design. Additionally, they provide a place of repose amid the bustle of a second-floor shopper circulation where customers can sit and observe ongoing activity. When balconies are conveniently located intermittently along a mall's thoroughfare without causing undue disruption to customer circulation, the owner/developer may not need to provide expanded areas for relaxation.

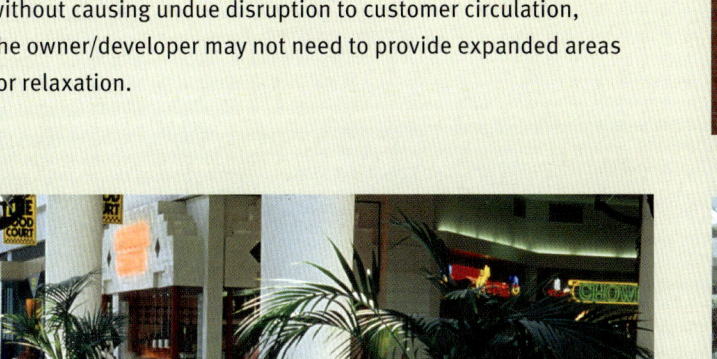

Bridges

Over the years, the shopping center has evolved to allow maximum visibility of merchant storefronts between shopping levels. Narrower bridges, strategically located to provide adequate cross-mall circulation, have replaced wide, heavy platforms to encourage merchant success. These lighter bridges, which customers walk on, create a zone of personal space that reinforces the overall architectural identity.

Skylights

No single element of a shopping center contributes greater definition to a space than its roof structure and skylight. Natural light, working hand in hand with structure, defines space to create a presence and quality that cannot be replicated artificially. Yet every region of the world is affected differently by its relationship to the solar environment.

168

Specialty Lighting
While providing ambient light for each shopping center, specialty lighting also creates an individuality that reinforces the architecture to give the building dramatic impact. This is the necessary and serious lighting that satisfies a center's basic illumination needs, but it also brings spaces alive, reinforcing their essential character and adding value to the space.

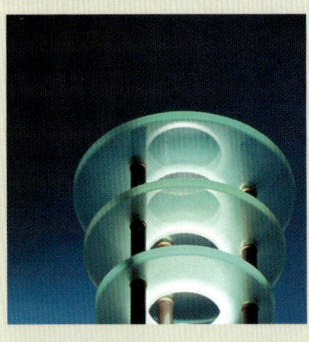

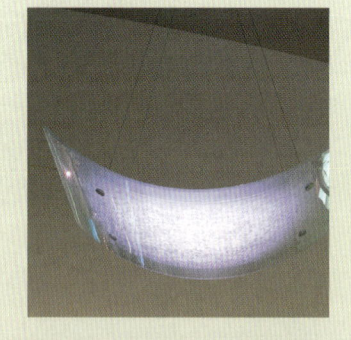

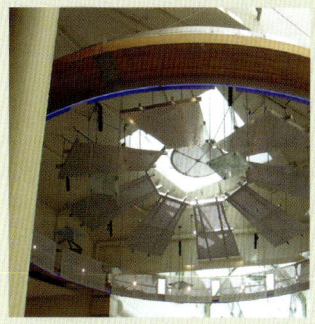

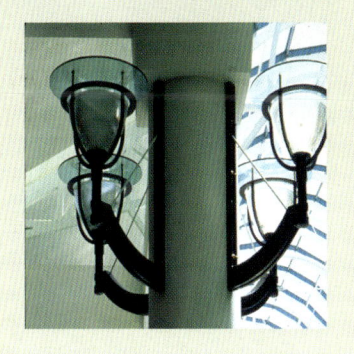

Decorative Lighting

In the absence of sunlit space or at night, decorative lighting acts as a counterpoint to a dark or muted environment, as it injects a sense of fantasy into the shopping experience. Judiciously applied, it enriches a shopping center and creates a special aura. Often playful and sometimes animated, it psychologically establishes obvious or subliminal interest.

Kiosks

In earlier generations of shopping centers, kiosks were temporary, as were the merchants who occupied them. The transient appearance conflicted with the overall fashion theme. By maintaining absolute control over the design of large and small kiosks, carts and other formats of specialty retail, a center can contribute to the ambience by placing these tenants in prominent areas. The kiosks can provide an intimate scale akin to streetscape furnishings. At the same time, their festive marketplace imagery adds a spontaneity that complements in-line retail shops.

Landscapes

In venues where a tradition of landscape maintenance exists and landscape specimens are plentiful, more conventional approaches provide soft, quiet places that contrast with the high-energy focus of retail complexes. Conventional plantings of trees, shrubs and colorful flowers provide a welcome respite from, and counterpoint to, retail activity. Trees are often planted directly in the ground with grates or underplantings, or in oversized pots, where space allows. Local specimens root the project in the regional context.

Architectural Landscapes

In many communities, the unavailability of appropriate landscape, the spatial demands, the costs of maintenance or the absence of natural light sources precludes the use of specimen trees within shopping centers. In such situations or when a more urban character is desired, the inclusion of highly architectural landscape elements is appropriate. This is a large vocabulary of garden-related elements, including trellises, arbors, column trees, pot rails and landscape troughs that can be introduced to create a sophisticated landscape presence, utilizing plant materials that are easy to maintain or replace.

Amenities

The furnishings in centers are immediately translatable from culture to culture. While styles and types of benches and chairs bear local nuances, everyone uses them. Amenities, including backed and backless benches, chairs, trash receptacles, ashtrays, drinking fountains, telephones and bicycle racks, are often crafted locally and are often based on more-expensive imported designs. These copies frequently perform less well than those that have been manufactured to meet stringent performance specifications, so the production and testing of alternate elements should be reviewed carefully.

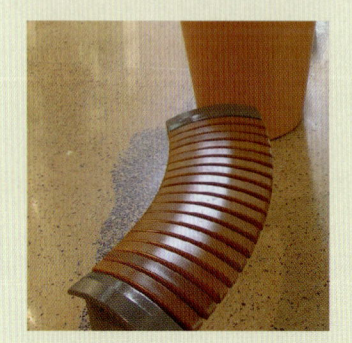

Fountains

Water is a design feature common to all cultures. Fountains, used for visual or audio impact, can be traditional in form or incorporated as a work of art and may be passive or interactive. While the latter poses maintenance and safety issues, interactive fountains are popular with young people and parents with children, who appreciate their entertainment value. However applied, fountains are visually popular with customers of all ages, as they create a sense of personal engagement that no other element produces.

Signage

The highly sophisticated signage systems of Europe and the playful and artistic approaches of North America contribute measurably to the quality of the retailing experience in those venues. Signage programs occasionally meet resistance in development projects in less industrialized countries based on the cost of design and because of limited resources for local fabrication and installation. Despite the difficulties, adequate signage can have significant bearing on the success of projects.

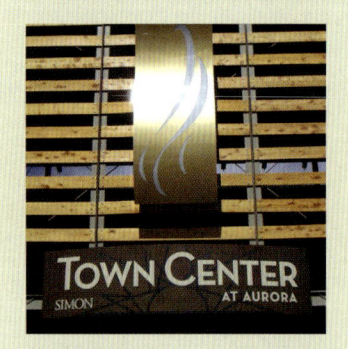

175

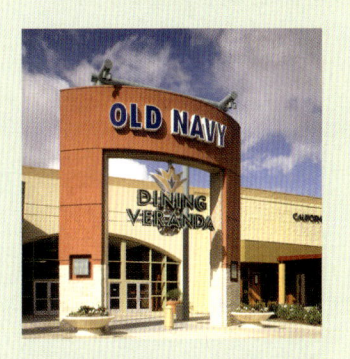

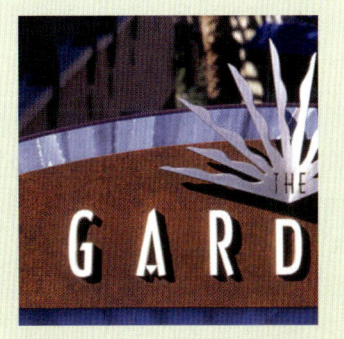

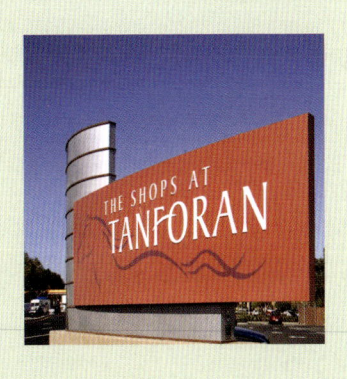

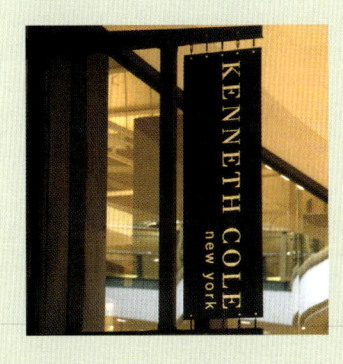

Environmental Graphics

Beyond functional signage systems, graphic design elements help to embellish the theme of a center down to the smallest detail, incorporating historic, cultural and regional references. These elements are playful and informative, educational and entertaining, colorful and functional. Yet they form a part of the entertaining vocabulary of a center that is no less important than landscaping or decorative lighting, as they recall the specific culture of a project, tie it to a specific place and allow the project to measurably separate itself from its competition in the consumer's eye.

176

177

178

Artwork

Art is a cultural asset with lasting community value. The public relations benefit from sponsoring and implementing an arts program, as well as the extended benefit of outreach programs that frequently engage primary and secondary schools, build an enduring two-way commitment. That relationship helps position a center as a member of the community it serves. In some cases, it is possible to rotate an arts program from one center to another.

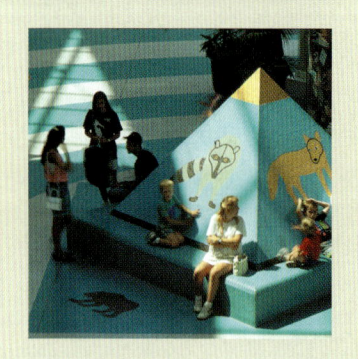

Information Systems and Directories

Graphic design begins with the directories, which not only communicate information to the visitor but also introduce the theme of the center. Functional, attractive, flexible and durable, directories are the formal greeting of a center. Technological innovation allows digital communications relative to the center, its programs and even its advertisements. They can also provide other useful community or promotional information. Individual pocket directories are often available in such locations.

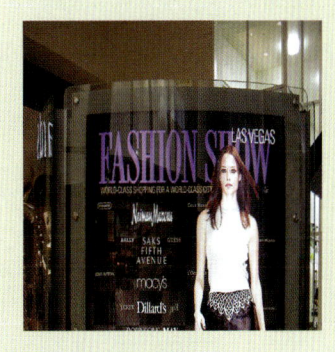

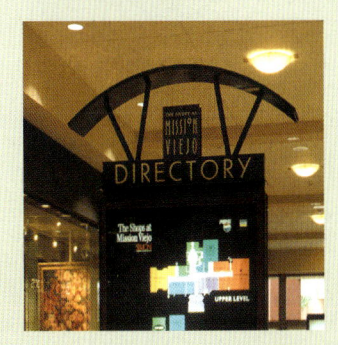

Other Items

There is a myriad of interactive elements and architectural details, from cornices to canopies and tree grates to flagpoles, that combine to create a rich ambience and an individual identity. Successful designs position a retail property comfortably within the context of its surrounding community. The very best shopping centers create a sense of place that fixes that center in the customer's mind as a special, specific place. Properly considered, these elements combine to define a shopping environment that will sustain itself through time.

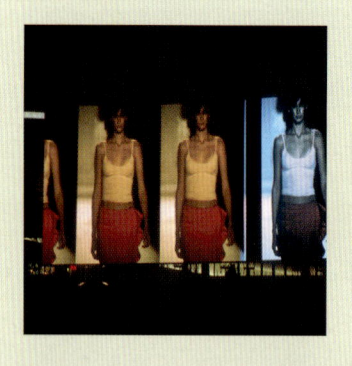

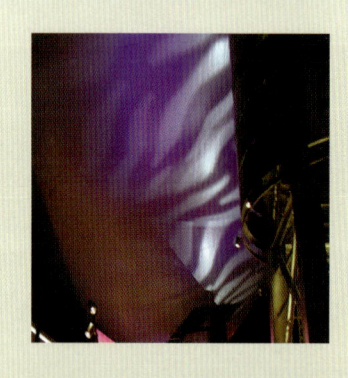

181

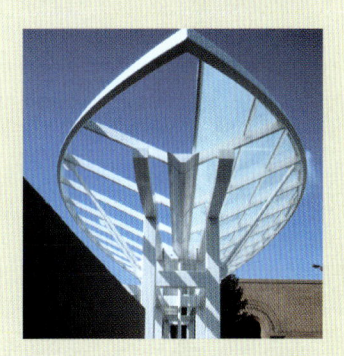

13. The Language of Open-Air Centers

WHEN DESIGNING OPEN-AIR shopping centers and retail districts—new Main Street and downtown-like developments—the language changes from that of enclosed centers as surely as it does when one flies from Los Angeles to Jakarta. In open-air projects, instead of entrances, there are gateways; rather than skylights, there are trellises; and where there were paving tiles, there are sidewalks with curbs, gutters and parking meters.

In an open-air center, all dimensional relationships are different than in an enclosed one, as it is critically important to create a sense of "authenticity," which often demands a height-to-width ratio of building to street that is uncommon in an enclosed one- or two-level mall. While a two- to six-story environment defines the community, a single-level retail environment within it must sustain the authentic scale. The point of departure for a Main Street or downtown project is rooted in the history of cities on every continent, with a genetic code that varies accordingly.

The Public Realm

Designing an open-air center begins with a social covenant, the need for harmony. The streets and sidewalks are the typical components of the public realm. Long the responsibility of city government's departments of planning, transportation and public works, they comprise the urban framework into which private- and public-sector owners erect separate buildings. Therefore, standards for constructing public right-of-ways were established for all elements contained within the domain of the public realm. Common hardscape materials were applied consistently throughout a village, town or city. Occasionally, the standard furnishings differed from street to street, recognizing different uses or establishing individual neighborhood identity; still, the standards remained. Over time, the standards have become more inventive, as cities seek to bring uniqueness to their communities. Following are examples of some of the many elements of the public realm, which, when combined, establish the framework for city building.

Streets

The streets play host to a limited, but important, group of elements that control vehicular traffic and protect the pedestrian when crossing from one side to the other. The important elements are:

- Paving: poured textured concrete, precast concrete, brick, stone, granite
- Crosswalks: painted concrete edge bands, distinctive pedestrian-scaled pavers
- Gutters: public works, standards or upgrades
- Utility and manhole covers: distinctive, cast-iron patterns, with symbolic words of identification
- Overhead lights: vehicular and pedestrian safety, unique for special cityscape zones
- Directional signage: street names, districts, directions, addresses

Sidewalks

Sidewalks provide the most immediate interface between the pedestrian and the streets in any city. Both play host to an array of elements, from the making of the sidewalk itself, to what is placed upon it, to what faces it as vertical facades. The three-dimensional definition of this outdoor zone is one of the most critical challenges of all, particularly in the making of Main Street or downtown multiblock centers. Among the elements requiring close attention are the following:

- Curbs
- Paving
- Streetlights
- Pot hangers
- Banner hangers
- Stoplights
- Stop signs
- Bus stop signs
- Bus stop structures
- Taxi stands
- Parking meters
- Street signs
- Bollards
- Tree grates
- Speakers
- Mailboxes
- Fire hydrants
- Pots
- Landscape guards
- Directional signage

The Private Realm

Harmony is a word from the Greek, a carpenter's term meaning joinery. It presupposes the similarity of elements, the singularity of ideas, the snugness found in a perfect fit.

Harmony or similarity of elements, the singularity of ideas is best represented in the public realm as the framework, which then supports, by contrast, dissonant architectural voices. However, the private realm is the place for differing styles. The private realm of shopfronts, then, can be individualized to the maximum and coexist against the common framework of the public realm. The private-realm components are:

Buildings

Perhaps more than any other contributing factor, the organization of building masses and the design of building facades will bring character and definition to every street, passage, alley, square, civic space and pathway. Here, the opportunity exists to explore the full range of creative personalities. At some additional cost, developers might replicate a historic environment, recalling imagery from the past. Or they may decide to build an entirely contemporary street and spend the construction budget on better materials. Alternatively, developers could do both and create the impression of a town constructed over several generations. Whatever the direction, the buildings will need to utilize the following elements:

- Building signage
- Tenant signage
- Address
- Marquees
- Canopies
- Awnings
- Trellises
- Mail
- Siamese connections
- Fire control

Spaces

Within the blocks, between groups of buildings, spaces—nodes of activities—create a relief from the urban imperative of retail shops, offices, hotels, dining venues and other services. Such moments of relief are themselves defined by the buildings that proscribe them, and the paths that lead to them. Whether plazas, squares or courtyards, they are further enhanced by the introduction of many elements that bring individuality and definition and enable or restrict one type of activity or another. Among the modifiers are the following:

- Gates
- Fences
- Band shells
- Wind chimes
- Wind socks
- Sun dials
- Fireplaces
- Memorials
- Ramps
- Stairs
- Steps
- Fountains
- Kiosks
- Paseos

Furnishings

To complete the urban composition, elements may be placed within the public realm's sidewalks and paseos or in the spaces and nodes of the private realm. Furnishings bring social definition to sidewalks and spaces, creating use and purpose. Some of these elements include:

- Benches
- Kiosks
- Carts
- Fountains
- Bicycle racks
- News racks
- Art
- Trash containers
- Flagpoles
- Public information

Taken together, the elements of open-air centers are no different than those that have existed for centuries in every culture throughout the world. They have simply been defined in a way that allows one to carefully assemble them in a manner that may be distinctive for each separate community and, in doing so, to build community itself.

Amenities

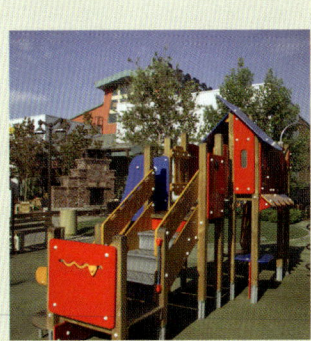

Addresses

Band Shells

Public Art

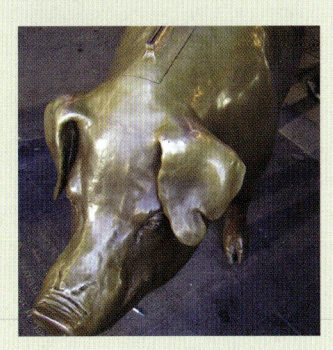

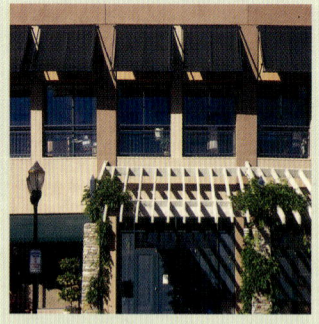

Awnings

Festival Signage

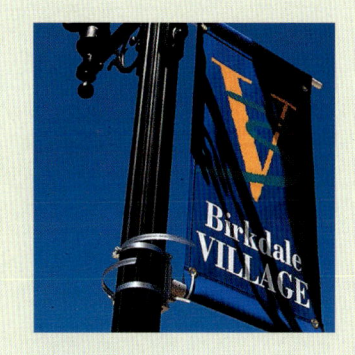

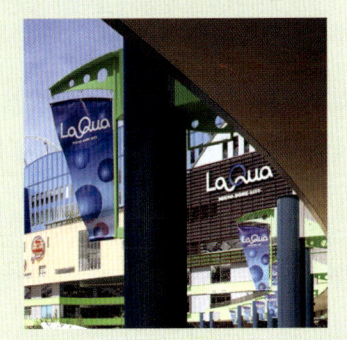

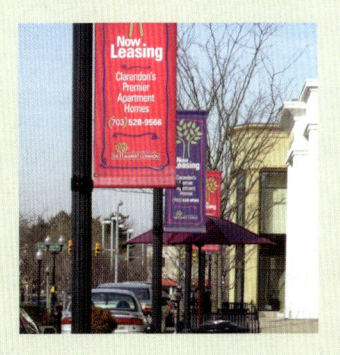

189

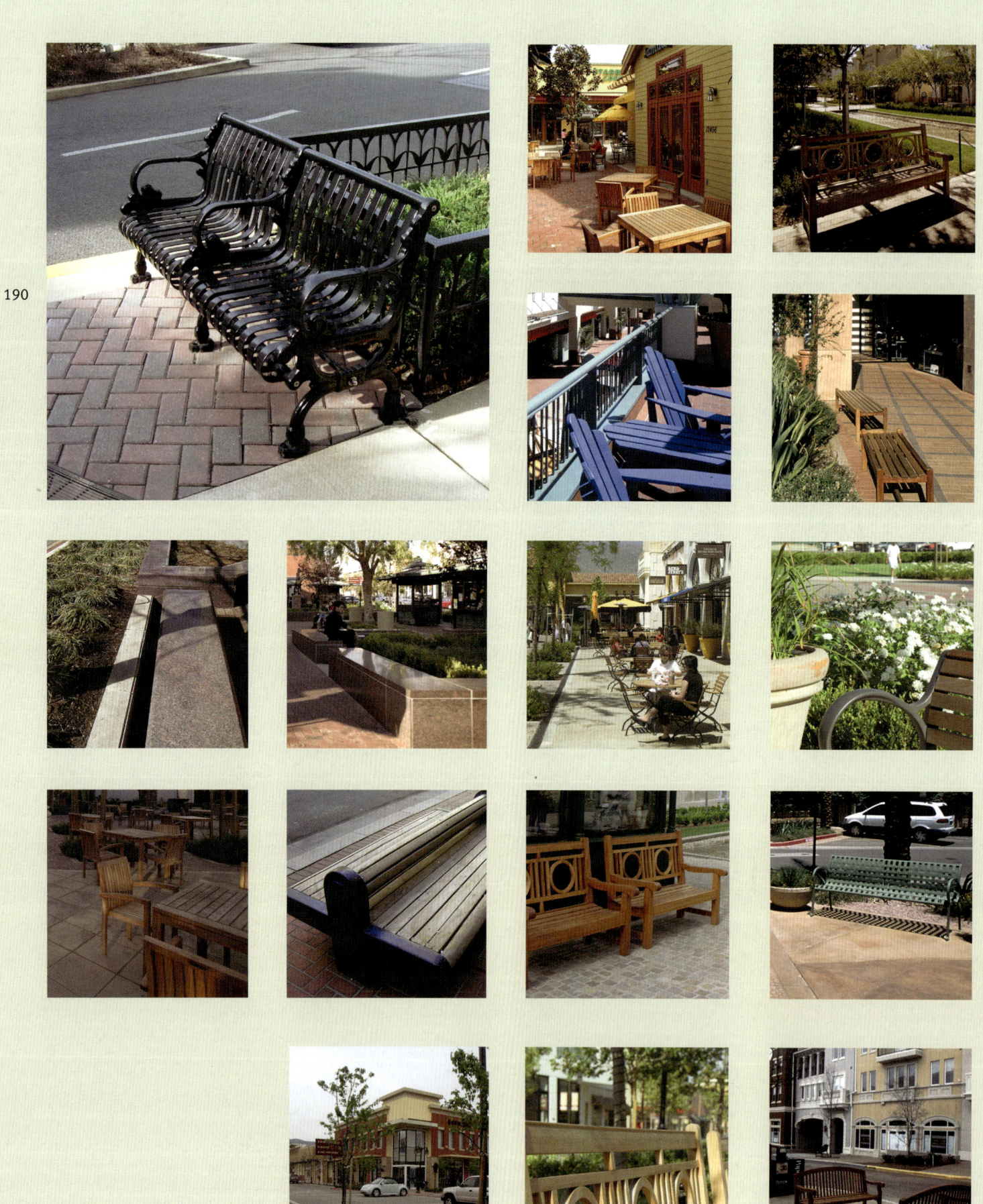

Benches

190

Bicycle Racks

Building Signage

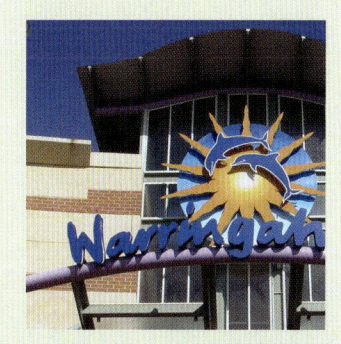

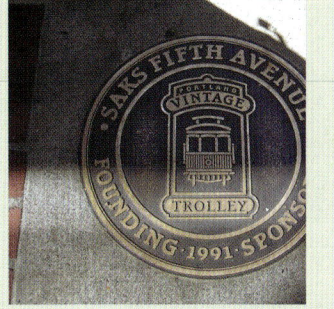

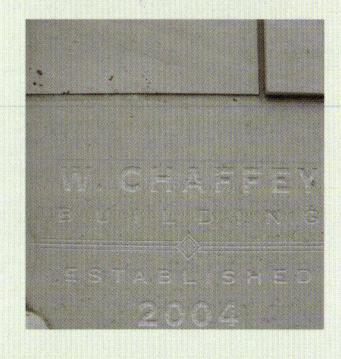

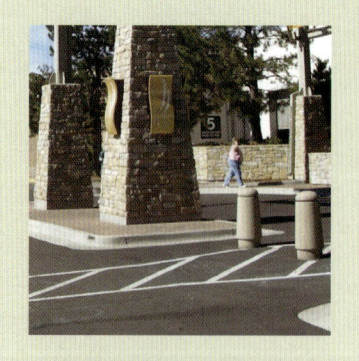

Bollards

Bus Stops

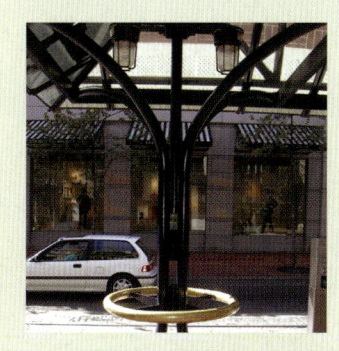

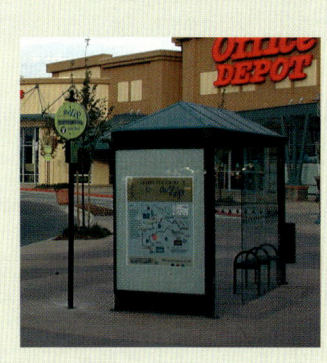

193

Trellises & Canopies

194

195

Carts

Wayfinding Graphics

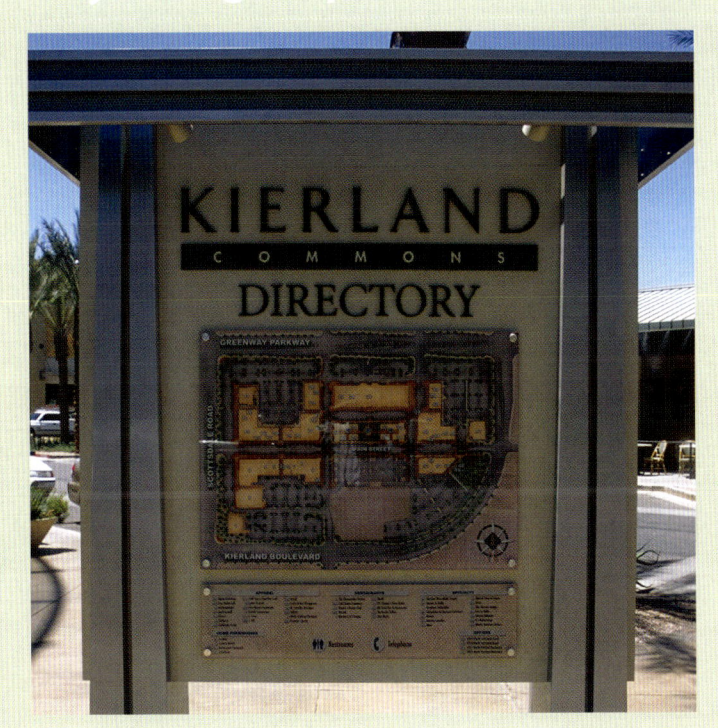

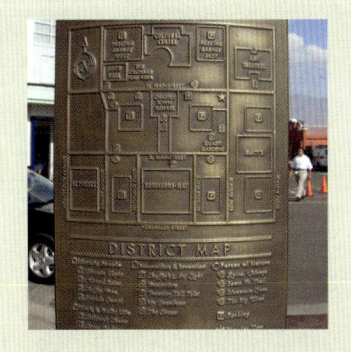

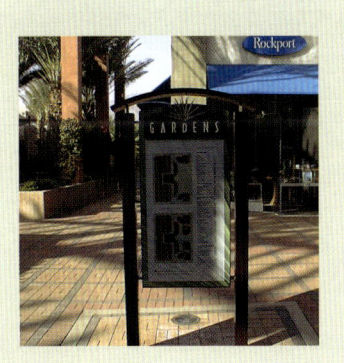

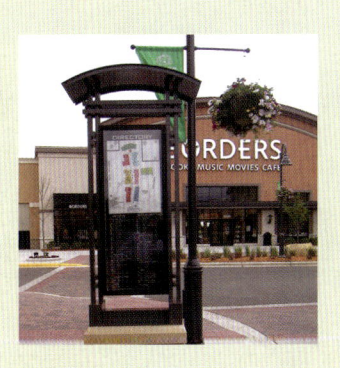

Paving & Crosswalks

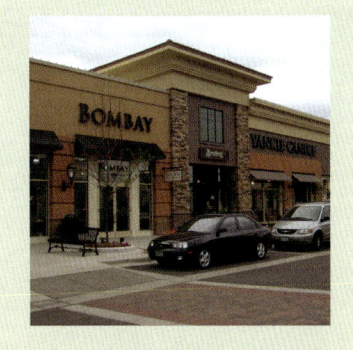

Escalators

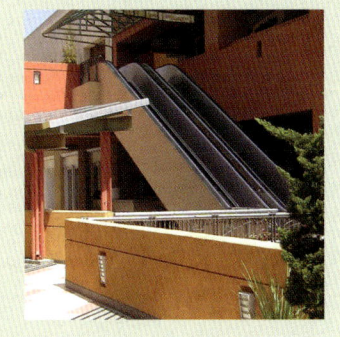

Environmental Graphics

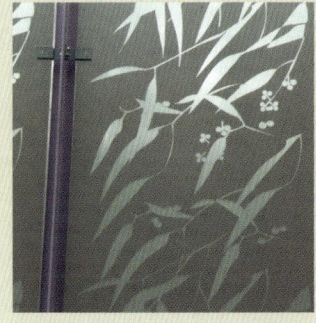

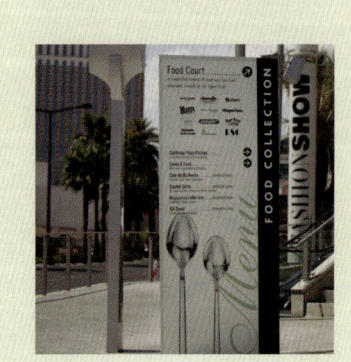

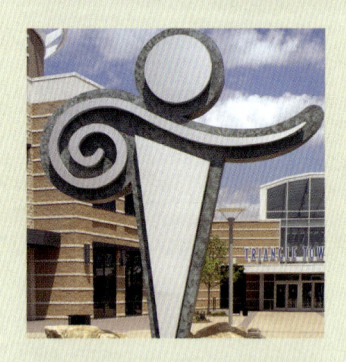

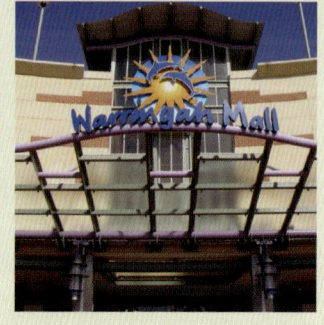

200

Fire Places

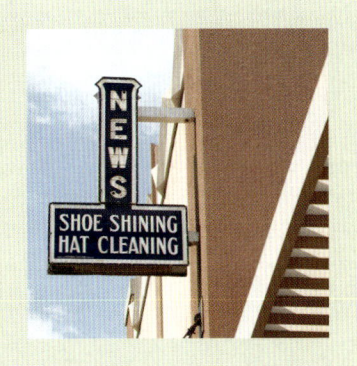

Fountains

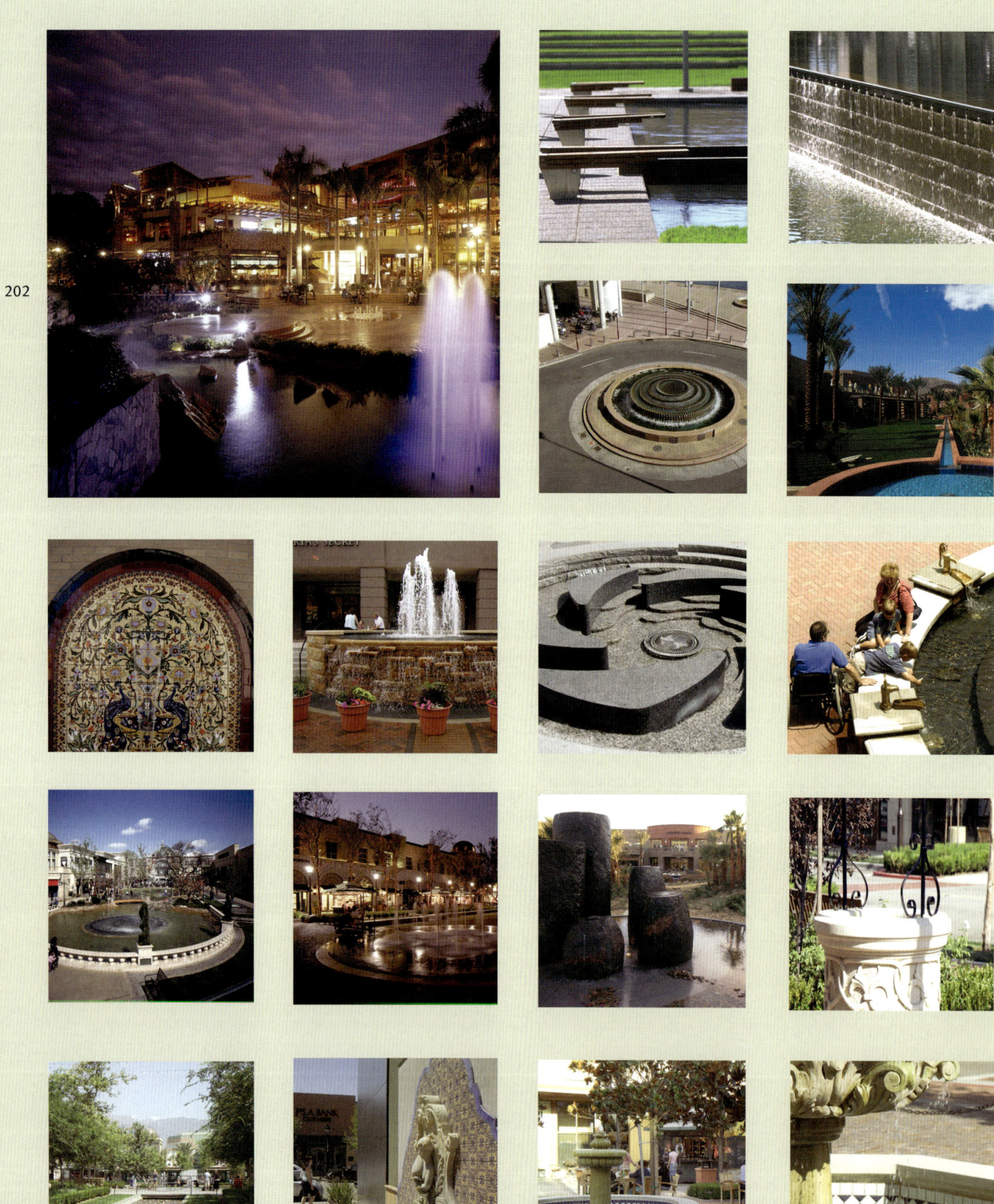

202

203

204

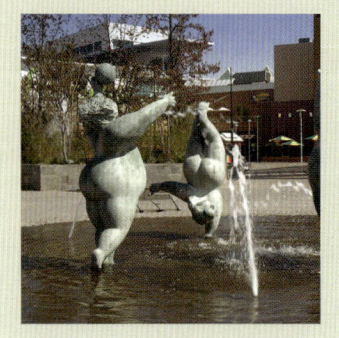

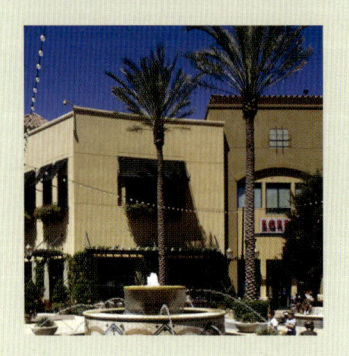

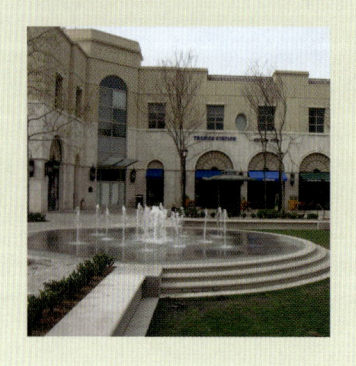

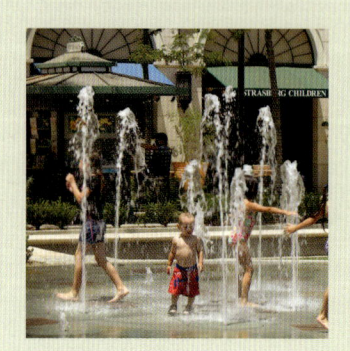

Guard Rails

Gutters

Kiosks

205

Landscape

206

207

208

209

Building Lights

211

Manhole Covers

212

Marquees

Commemorative Graphics

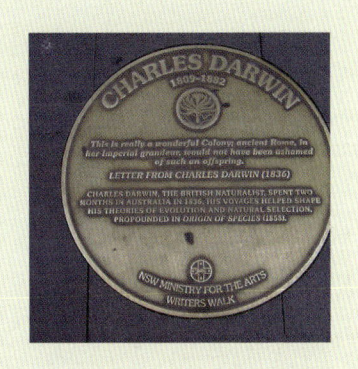

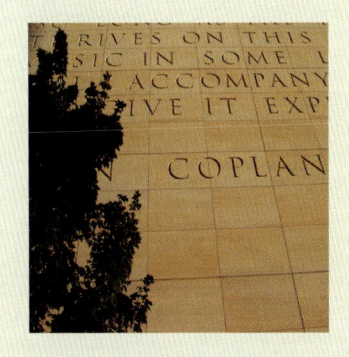

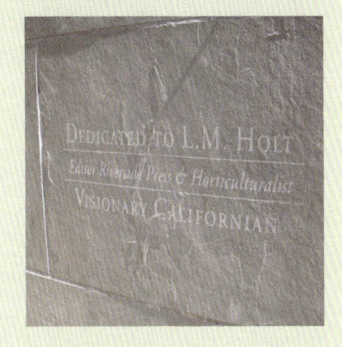

Architectural Details

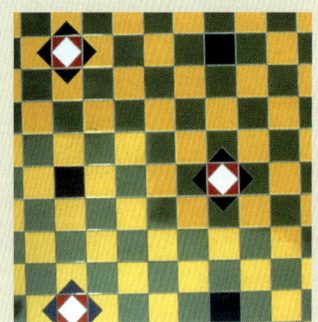

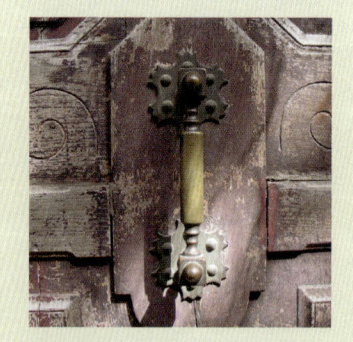

215

216

217

News Racks

14. Building Smarter: Sustainable Design

IF THERE IS ONE thing that is consistent in the retail development and design sectors, it is change. It has always been the hallmark of retailing, as retail sales thrive on change. This factor has driven sales, profits, rents and development direction. The competitive retailer is focused on weekly merchandising adjustments, as bar-code tracking has been tied to product delivery and purchasing.

Buildings were initially designed to accommodate slower, but predictable, change. As was done historically in the passages, arcades and gallerias of Europe, the highly disciplined shell accommodated either a standard shopfront or individualized tenant fitouts. Within this context, tenant reimaging tended to occur on the average of every seven years, as did department store fitout renovations. This change was anticipated and provided for in order to prevent merchants being perceived as stale.

One of the most recent and significant changes is environmental responsibility, sometimes referred to as *sustainable design*. This approach is also known as green building, or environmentally friendly. It has to do with all aspects of site selection, site planning, building design, integration with nature and the contextual environment and the sensitive use of natural resources.

The United States General Services Administration (GSA), the single largest landlord in the United States, is achieving public buildings of exceptionally high design standard, while satisfying client/tenant needs. The GSA is now demanding that the United States Green Building Council apply its LEED™ rating system to certify buildings in all of the projects it commissions. Following this example, many state governments, which get federal funding for public projects, are also requiring LEED™ certification for the buildings they commission.

It stands to reason that if in the United States, the federal, state, county and local government sectors are requiring LEED™ certification for the buildings they commission for themselves, in due course, they will likely require that all private-sector buildings also comply. Codes and standards, which reflect the principles of sustainable design, are in formation. The groundswell has arrived.

The LEED™ Certification Program Requirements

The United States Green Building Council LEED™ certification program is essentially a point system, with certain compulsory requirements, to assure that each design is complying to certain minimum standards, with the potential to reach substantially higher goals. Many countries have equivalent systems, but for purposes of this discussion, the LEED™ certification system will be utilized. The Green Building Council breaks the point system into several categories. They are, simplistically put, as follows:

1. A *LEED™ Accredited Professional*. This is a person who has passed an examination on the subject and is required to participate in the design process and to monitor the options and design choices to assure that reasonable decisions are made.
2. *Sustainable sites*. Under the category of sustainable sites, points are awarded for careful site selection, urban redevelopment projects, brownfield development, integration of alternative-transportation systems, proper storm-water management systems, and reduced heat islands and light pollution.
3. *Water efficiency*. Dealing with water efficiency, a sensitive approach to water-efficient landscaping, use of innovative wastewater technologies and water use reduction are considered.
4. *Energy and atmosphere*. In the category of energy and atmosphere, building systems commissioning (monitoring to assure delivery of what has been designed and specified) is essential, along with minimum energy use, chlorofluorocarbon (CFC) reduction, optimization of energy performance and use of renewable energy.
5. *Materials and resources*. Materials and resources decisions are an essential part of the formula, including the storage/collection of recyclables on-site, building reuse where possible, a system of construction waste management, resource reuse, recycled content, use of local/regional materials produced within 500 miles and the utilization of rapidly renewable materials.

6. *Indoor Environmental Quality (IEQ)*. IEQ suggests minimum IEQ performance, environmental tobacco smoke control, increased ventilation effectiveness, a construction IEQ management plan, use of low-emitting materials, indoor chemical and pollutant control, assuring thermal comfort and proper consideration of daylight and views.
7. *Innovation and design process*. Lastly, innovation and design process offers a wide-open opportunity for architects and their developer clients to pursue unconventional concepts that may be suggested by the contextual conditions.

All of this may seem daunting, but when placed side by side with the evaluation of contextual forces discussed in previous chapters, it is a rather straightforward approach. Yet there are challenges with retail projects, mostly stemming from an entrenched position coming from the general direction of a developer's investment strategy.

Challenges to Sustainable Design

1. The financing structure of the deal can complicate the proper consideration of an alternative product type. As an example, many capital-market sources fund simple deals, not innovative or complicated ones, usually focusing on retail, office, residential or hotel, but not a mix of several of them.

2. Capital first costs are always a blinding factor. Unlike development in the public, corporate or academic sectors, commercial developers generally want to keep initial costs as low as reasonable, while assuring the quality of the investment intended. Life-cycle costs are rarely considered with any seriousness.

3. Another common unknown is the duration of ownership. If a developer is building a project to hold in a portfolio for decades, the developer's decisions should be based on not only first costs, but on operating expenses as well. But if the project is being developed for purposes of a relatively quick sale, then first costs are what matters most to a developer.

4. Even the calculation of total rent is critical to the decision-making process. Rent is generally comprised of two elements—a formal annual rent-per-square-foot and a Common Area Maintenance (CAM) charge—to compensate the owner for maintaining the public areas of the project as well as other costs. Among other factors, the tenant will evaluate the total of these two costs and compare it to other competing venues when making a real estate decision. The value of the property asset, however, is a multiple of the rent role, not the CAM charge. So if the operating CAM costs were to be reduced significantly, then the actual per square foot rent could increase proportionally, while maintaining the same competitive total rental rate. In short, one can maximize the value of an asset by making it more sustainable. It makes sense to be energy-efficient and environmentally sensitive not only from a civic-minded point of view, but also from an economic one.

Centers with Sustainable Design

So the inevitable question arises, how does one measure the return on investment (ROI) on sustainable design in the retail development industry? One only needs to look at the performance of the projects identified here.

The following are six examples of projects designed to sustainable design standards, without significant construction budget implications. Five are completed projects, and one has been approved for implementation by its jurisdictional agencies. A quick review of each, along with some bullet points of areas in which they excelled, is worthy of note.

Fashion Valley Shopping Center, San Diego, CA, United States

Fashion Valley, which utilized an existing structure while building above it, realized a substantial shopper increase by virtue of recognizing the welcoming nature of the natural environment and capitalizing on it. Continuously rated number one in a regionwide customer popularity poll, the sales-per-square-foot are running considerably above the predecessor building, far ahead of the competition, and among the five percent best-performing centers in the United States. And the second-floor sales are outperforming first-floor sales, illustrating that sustainable principles applied insightfully can yield positive financial results.

Sustainable Design Factors

Site selection and development:
- The reuse of a previously developed site for intensified retail and leisure uses helps preserve undeveloped land and reduces pressures toward urban sprawl.
- The expansion of parking through the use of multilevel parking structures places more than one-half of the car parking under cover, reducing the heat island effect of large surface lots.
- The storm water management plan for the site is designed in coordination with regional plans to handle a 500-year flood event at this site.

Development density and community connectivity:
- The development of a multimodal transportation hub makes the project an important linkage point between automobile, light rail, bus, pedestrian and bicycle routes with the effect of reducing auto trips to the site.

Water efficiency:
- The landscape design incorporating indigenous and adapted plant varieties and efficient irrigation systems reduces water consumed for irrigation to one-half that of conventional practice.
- The use of low-flow faucets and low-flush toilet fixtures along with motion sensors substantially reduces water consumption.

Energy efficiency:
- Accomplishing the expansion of the existing center while the center continued its normal operating hours preserved business, jobs, and services for the community and reduced auto trips to remote shopping alternatives.
- Developing the common public areas as open-air rather than enclosed eliminated the energy otherwise needed for air-conditioning and ventilation of this volume.
- The use of high walls in narrow spaces, trellises and landscaping provides shading to temper the common areas and reduce solar heat loads on the enclosed buildings.
- Locally sourcing most building materials (within 500 miles of a project) reduced transportation energy consumed and created less pollution caused by transportation.

Material resources: Reuse of existing building and retail build-over
- A vertical expansion (build-over) allowed for creation of new second level while maintaining (in-use) the existing one-level shopping center.
- The embodied energy of the existing construction materials was preserved, maintaining 95% of existing walls, floors and roof.
- The reuse of existing building materials meant that they did not need to be replaced with new building materials, thus reducing consumption and diverting waste from landfill.

Queen Ka'ahumanu Center, Kahului, Maui, Hawaii, United States

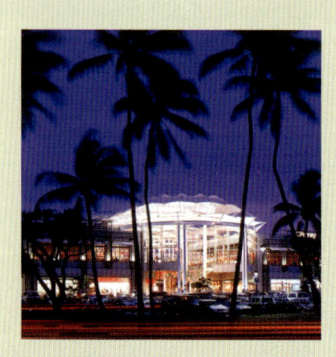

Queen Ka'ahumanu Center experienced lower operational costs compared to enclosed regional centers. Implementing concepts such as recaptured rainwater further reduced the operational costs. As locals recognized a cultural tie with the project, the public relations value that came from the community's verbal network created an island-wide acceptance of the project that surpassed expectations.

Sustainable Design Factors

Site selection and development:
- The reuse and repurposing of a previously industrial site for intensified retail and leisure uses helps preserve undeveloped land and reduces pressures toward urban sprawl.

Water efficiency:
- All storm water is captured on-site and is then used on-site or passed to the local aquifer through infiltration.
- Storm water is used to irrigate the landscaping, eliminating the use of potable water for irrigation

Energy efficiency through the use of Teflon-coated fiberglass skylight roof:
- The high heat reflectivity of the fabric roof (75%) creates a shaded, natural lit interior that requires no air-conditioning in the common public areas.
- High, visible light transmission of the fabric roof (75%) means only minimal artificial lighting is needed throughout the daylight hours.
- Highly reflective roof materials minimize heat island effect of buildings.
- The layered and open-flutter sail concept of the roof provides natural ventilation and access to views of the mountains and ocean. It also provides a relationship to local landscape and cultural traditions.

Material resources: Reuse of existing building, retail build-over and storage building relocation
- A vertical expansion (build-over) allowed for creation of new second level while maintaining (in-use) the existing one-level shopping center.
- The embodied energy of the existing construction materials was preserved, maintaining 95% of existing walls, floors and roof.
- The reuse of existing building materials meant that they did not need to be replaced with new building materials, thus reducing consumption and diverting waste from landfill.
- Relocation of a storage warehouse was accomplished through disassembly and reassembly on-site.
- The embodied energy of the existing construction materials was preserved.

Material resources: New construction
- The premanufactured roof system materials were computer cut in a factory and no excess material was delivered to the site; therefore, there was no wastage to remove.
- The premanufactured roof system allowed for a three-month shorter construction schedule, reducing the duration of disturbance to the surrounding neighborhood.
- Installing the premanufactured roof system reduced the amount of noise generated from the site compared to more conventional building techniques.

The Gardens on El Paseo, Palm Desert, California, United States

The Gardens on El Paseo, as an open-air center in a very arid desert context, achieves the highest amount of pedestrian traffic among its competition in the extended trade area of the Coachella Valley. Sales-per-square-foot substantially exceed expectations, and the positive response from both resident and tourist customers reflects the value achieved from accepting a challenging natural environment and transforming it successfully with sensitive design.

Sustainable Design Factors

Site selection and development:
- Storm water runoff retention reduces impacts on local infrastructure and passes most storm water to the local aquifer through on-site infiltration.
- The heat island effect is minimized through pervious paving and shading of hardscape surfaces.
- Highly reflective roof materials are used to minimize the heat island effect of buildings.

Development density and community connectivity:
- As an urban infill project the center continues and completes an existing shopping district.
- The project contributes much-needed shared parking facilities to the local shopping district.

Water efficiency:
- The landscape design incorporating indigenous and adapted plant varieties and efficient irrigation systems reduces water consumed for irrigation to one-half that of conventional practice.
- The use of low-flow faucets and low-flush toilet fixtures along with motion sensors substantially reduces water consumption.

Energy efficiency: Use of traditional desert-climate mitigation strategies to ease the effect of temperatures that can reach 115° F (42° C)
- Developing the common public areas as open air, rather than enclosed, eliminated the energy otherwise needed to condition and ventilate this volume.
- The use of high walls in narrow spaces, trellises and landscaping provide shading to temper the common areas and reduce solar heat loads on the enclosed buildings.
- Palm bosque set in decomposed granite (pervious paving) increases permeability and reduces heat island effect.
- Pavers are set in sand (pervious paving) and can be watered down to create an evaporative cooling effect.
- The "psychological" use of a small amount of water in a highly visible way creates a sense of relief from the desert heat.
- Development of a parking structure places over one-half of parking under cover, reducing the heat island effect.

Material resources:
- The majority of materials are local in origin, sourced within a 500-mile radius of the project, reducing transportation energy consumed and pollution created by having to bring materials to the site.
- Integral color stucco is resistant to airborne dust and desert winds, meaning less frequent replacement of building finishes over time.

Botany Town Centre, Auckland, New Zealand

Botany Town Center carefully integrated its current and planned adjacent residential and retail neighbors with its sensitivity to the spiritual values of the indigenous people. As a result, the center has seen very positive customer acceptance in the development of subsequent phases along with positive sales figures.

Sustainable Design Factors

Site selection and development:
- Integration with public transit: rerouting of bus lines, with bus stops and a taxi stand located on-site with shelters provided by the center.
- Generous bicycle storage with showers and lockers on-site for employees.
- Minimized heat island effect, with pervious paving and extensive shading on hardscape surfaces.
- Restored native habitat through stylized use of native plant materials at the edges of the property that abut local nature preserves.
- Light-pollution reduction: no direct-beam light is projected into the night sky or onto neighboring properties.
- Management of storm water runoff quantity and quality to predevelopment levels with use of constructed ponds and wetlands.
- A portion of the site is dedicated to a rare flax plant arboretum maintained by local native Maori people for use in their traditional crafts and ceremonies.

Development density and community connectivity:
- As a mixed-use center: office, retail, entertainment, dining and community services—such as public meeting rooms, a branch library and a police substation—are all provided.
- Multimodal linkages to residential/civic/retail functions have been created.
- The project provides for the creation of civic event space for community functions.

Water efficiency:
- The landscape design incorporating indigenous and adapted plant varieties and efficient irrigation systems reduces water consumed for irrigation to less than one-half that of conventional practice.
- The site perimeter zones adjacent to established land preserves are developed with only native plant material (restoring and connecting native habitat). The irrigation in these areas is temporary and is designed to be removed after the establishing period.
- The use of low-flow faucets and low-flush toilet fixtures along with motion sensors substantially reduces water consumption.

Energy efficiency:
- Developing most of the common public areas as open air rather than enclosed eliminated the energy otherwise needed to condition and ventilate these volumes.
- The use of displacement ventilation in enclosed common areas greatly reduces cooling energy required to condition and ventilate these spaces. It allowed for use of 100% outdoor air to condition these spaces for most of the operating hours of the center.

Material resources:
- All materials were sourced within New Zealand, reducing the transportation energy consumed and pollution created in bringing construction materials to the site.
- All materials were selected with a preference for low-VOC-emitting materials, and the use of certified wood.
- Significant artworks were produced by local artists in celebration of the native landscape of New Zealand and the multiethnic culture it supports.

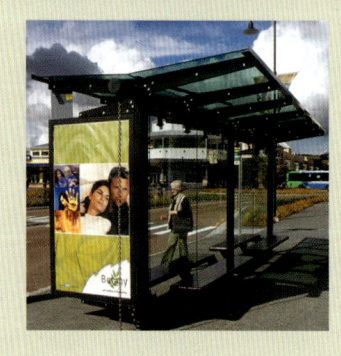

The Shops at Tanforan,
San Bruno, California, United States

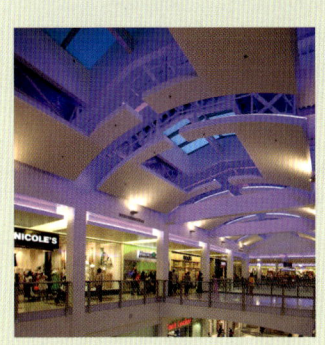

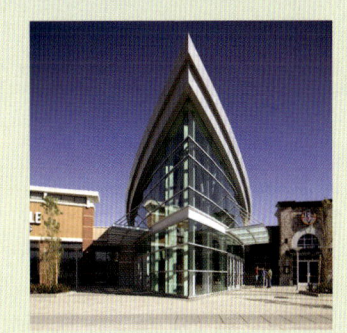

The Shops at Tanforan, utilizing highly sustainable design along with passive and active technologies, was able to achieve lower operating costs, which translated into a higher property valuation. As a greater proportion of the total rent was ultimately assigned to actual occupancy rent rather than common area maintenance charges, the book value of the resulting investment demonstrated that a sustainable design strategy was not only ethically strong but also financially viable.

Sustainable Design Factors

Site selection and development:
- Public transit linkage: the BART subway station and bus station/hub for multiple city lines are adjacent to the site, and taxi stands are located on the property.
- Linkages to local pedestrian and bicycle paths are created and bicycle storage facilities are provided.
- Shading and the use of pervious paving materials reduces the heat island effect of hardscape areas.
- Highly reflective roof materials minimize the heat island effect of buildings.
- Light pollution is reduced, as there is no direct-beam light into the night sky or adjacent properties.

Water efficiency:
- Existing mature trees were maintained and native plants and water-efficient irrigation were installed, greatly reducing water use for irrigation.
- The use of low-flow faucets and low-flush toilet fixtures along with motion sensors substantially reduces water consumption.

Energy efficiency:
- Refurbishment and upgrade of an existing efficient chilled-water mechanical system provided a refrigerant-free cooling system for the project.
- Lighting system designed to be 25% more efficient than California Energy Code requirements saves substantial cooling energy as well. Most cooling load is met using 100% outside air most of the time. Daylight sensors also turn off mall lights when daylight provides ample indoor lighting levels.

Material resources:
- Adaptive reuse of building shell and structure preserved the embodied energy of the materials in the existing construction, maintaining 75% of existing walls, floors and roof, thus diverting waste from landfill.
- Reuse of materials on-site: concrete from selective building demolition was crushed and reused as base material under new slabs. Asphalt from parking areas removed, restored and re-used to resurface parking lots.
- All interior materials selected comply with low VOC standards used in the LEED rating system.
- All waste materials from demolition and construction were taken off-site for sorting, and 74% of the total volume was recycled, diverting it from landfill.

Les Portes de Gascogne, Toulouse, France

This project, still in the design stages, has nonetheless been planned with all the guiding principles of sustainable design projects.

Sustainable Design Factors

Site selection and development:
- Project developed to serve as a regional public multimodal transportation hub.
- Management of storm water runoff quantity and quality to predevelopment levels with use of constructed ponds and wetlands.
- Storm water is retained, filtered and reused in evaporative cooling.
- Storm water is retained and used for all landscape irrigation, eliminating the use of potable water for irrigation.

Development density and community connectivity:
- Mixed use: office, retail, entertainment, dining and community services—such as public meeting rooms, a branch library, child care and a police sub-station—concentrate services and reduce the generation of single-purpose auto trips in the region.
- Multimodal linkages to residential/civic/retail functions reduce auto trip generation.
- Creation of a civic event space for community functions strengthens the sense of community.

Energy efficiency:
- The development of common public areas as covered but open spaces without air-conditioning greatly reduces total energy consumption otherwise associated with cooling and ventilating these large volumes of space.
- Solar and geothermal heat are harvested and stored in the building mass. Openings are protected to reduce summer solar gain, while maximizing winter gain.
- Building orientation and the position and development of openings achieves management of local wind conditions and supports natural ventilation.
- Night flushing with 100% outdoor air reduces the cooling load the following day.

Material resources:
- All materials are sourced locally and selected for low embodied energy, recycled content and the ability to be recycled at the end of use. This supports the local economy while reducing energy-related impacts on the atmosphere from the transportation of building materials.

Design innovation:
- "La Grande Serre" serves as civic city room for public events, promoting a sense of community.
- Parking lots and parking space are used as a closed-loop water use and treatment system.

Lessons in Sustainable Design

The success of those who have taken the initiative to embrace sustainable, energy-efficient, responsible resource utilization, and contextually and culturally sensitive design can serve as inspiration for future retail center designers. In order to get in front of the curve, protect existing assets and be a player in new ventures, consider the following:

1. Learn the local context. Understand the forces that affect a particular site. These include natural forces, geographic forces, historic human forces, physical forces, economic forces, cultural forces and political forces.

2. Embrace sustainable design as the friend that it can be. Become knowledgeable on the subject. Change your measurement standards of return on investment.

3. Design buildings and communities to be responsive to change and to be transformative over time, not as caricatures of another time.

4. Always reaffirm a community's sense of self.

5. Look to history. See what models have sustained themselves over centuries.

Seek to gain public trust and positive public opinion. The retail development community has contributed so much to the cities and towns in which its members develop—temporary and permanent jobs, taxes, infrastructure improvements, civic uses and spaces and convenient and safe environments. Some of the industry has committed to permanently embracing sustainably designed projects, and they are likely to be the first in line.

Conclusion: Context, Culture and Community

It seems quite clear that the holistic definition of context needs to be carefully and comprehensively understood, embraced and responded to in the making of place. The differences that bring distinction to one environment, differentiating it from another, are critical and not incidental. The myriad of contextual forces that are due proper consideration and design response will inform not only the design process but also the resulting design that responds to these forces. Each place will necessarily be defined distinctly from others and, in so being, will form the framework for supporting community preferences.

In response to the full range of physical contextual forces, culture has emerged again, distinctively different from continent to continent, nation to nation, region to region, village to village and even neighborhood to neighborhood. These cultural manifestations should be celebrated, as they further inform the development and design process. Every social structure exhibits its values and thrives when the places of community encourage the celebration of those values.

What will come from the acceptance of these myriad of contextually and culturally specific local voices and the resulting projects is that each place will benefit from an imbuing sense of community. Building community may be the highest value a development can achieve.

At the end of the day, community begets community. And, no greater aspiration can better support successful 21st Century retail centers.